John Bunyan deserves to
Pilgrim's Progress and *H*
sixty volumes. His lack o ... have added to
the suspicion that he does not rank among the greatest theologians, but this is a grave mistake. Erudite studies of Bunyan exist that demonstrate his wide knowledge and expertise in some of the most controversial theological topics. But we are in need of an accessible summary of the man and his writings that demonstrates Bunyan's vast contribution to Reformed experiential theology. This volume fills that gap by focusing on Bunyan's understanding of the fear of God that lies at the heart of his theology. A superb achievement.

—**Derek W. H. Thomas**, Senior Minister, First Presbyterian Church, Columbia, South Carolina

We have come to expect fine introductions to the Puritans from Joel Beeke, and this book does not disappoint. Here we get to see both the life and heart of John Bunyan, and through them we enjoy a rich, sensitive, and well-applied exposition of an important and much-neglected theme: the fear of the Lord. May God use this book to stir up a new generation of Bunyans who fear God and not man.

—**Michael Reeves**, President, Union School of Theology, Oxford, England

The deep admiration of that remarkable theologian John Owen for the ministry of his fellow Puritan John Bunyan is good reason why we today need to read and treasure Bunyan, and this new overview of Bunyan's works is a very helpful guide to that end. Using the unifying thread of the fear of God—one in which the Puritans have much to teach us—Beeke and Smalley take the reader through the core of Bunyan's corpus and whet the reader's appetite to plunge afresh into Bunyan's works.

—**Michael A. G. Haykin**, Professor of Church History and Biblical Spirituality, The Southern Baptist Theological Seminary, Louisville, Kentucky

Israelite midwives exhibited it, the psalms are full of it, wisdom requires it, Jesus emphasized it, the apostles encouraged it—and yet few things are more feared in contemporary Christianity than . . . the fear of God. In this timely book, Joel Beeke and Paul Smalley show how the fear of God was, in contrast, the heartbeat of John Bunyan, one of the most loved and admired of all Christians and the author of the all-time best selling Christian book. Here is proof—if any is needed—to confirm C. H. Spurgeon's famous comment on Bunyan: "Prick him anywhere—his blood is Bibline, the very essence of the Bible flows from him." Read these pages and you will learn the truth that "they love thee little, if at all, who do not fear thee much; if love is thine attraction, Lord, fear is thy very touch."

—**Sinclair B. Ferguson**, Dean, Doctor of Ministry program, Ligonier Academy of Biblical and Theological Studies, Sanford, Florida

JOHN BUNYAN *and the* GRACE *of* FEARING GOD

JOEL R. BEEKE
& PAUL M. SMALLEY

P.O. BOX 817 • PHILLIPSBURG • NEW JERSEY 08865-0817

Italics within Scripture quotations indicate emphasis added.

Printed in the United States of America

Library of Congress Cataloging-in-Publication Data

Names: Beeke, Joel R., 1952- author.
Title: John Bunyan and the grace of fearing God / Joel R. Beeke and Paul M. Smalley.
Description: Phillipsburg : P&R Publishing, 2016. | Includes bibliographical references.
Identifiers: LCCN 2016033921| ISBN 9781629952048 (pbk.) | ISBN 9781629952055 (epub) | ISBN 9781629952062 (mobi)
Subjects: LCSH: Bunyan, John, 1628-1688. | Dissenters, Religious--England--Biography. | Christian biography--England--Biography.
Classification: LCC PR3331 .B44 2016 | DDC 285/.9092 [B] --dc23
LC record available at https://lccn.loc.gov/2016033921

To Michael Barrett,
a great friend and colleague,
the best God-fearing academic dean and OT scholar
a seminary president could ever hope for.
"Behold, that thus shall the man be blessed that
feareth the LORD" (Ps. 128:4).

—Joel R. Beeke

To my dear wife, Dawn.
"A woman who fears the Lord is to be praised" (Prov. 31:30).

And to my three beloved children, Levi, Elizabeth, and Michael.
"As a father shows compassion to his children,
so the Lord shows compassion to those who fear him" (Ps. 103:13).

—Paul M. Smalley

What a weighty and great grace
this grace of the holy fear of God is.

—John Bunyan

Contents

Foreword

Few individuals have influenced this world for Jesus Christ more broadly than the renowned Puritan figure John Bunyan. In the nineteenth century, it was said that virtually every English house possessed two books: the *Authorized Version* of the Bible and Bunyan's *The Pilgrim's Progress*. If such a claim is even remotely true, it must be acknowledged that Bunyan exerted an extraordinary influence in that part of the English-speaking world. This far-reaching impact, though, was not restricted to his motherland. Through his gifted pen on the printed page, the spiritual legacy of Bunyan has reached around the globe.

Bunyan lived during the golden era of the Puritans, in one of the godliest generations ever assembled on the stage of human history. J. I. Packer has compared the Puritans to "California's Redwoods," giants in the forest of Christianity.[1] J. C. Ryle asserted that, in power as preachers, expositors, and writers, "the Puritans in their day were second to none."[2] The Puritans were devoted men and women within the Church of England, in the sixteenth and seventeenth centuries,

1. J. I. Packer, *A Quest for Godliness: The Puritan Vision of the Christian Life* (Wheaton, IL: Crossway, 1990), 11.

2. John Charles Ryle, *Facts and Men: Being Pages from English Church History, between 1553 and 1683* (London: William Hunt, 1882), xviii.

who sought to purify its doctrine and worship as well as their own lives. In a broader sense, the Puritan spirit also animated the Non-Conformist movement outside the national church. Bunyan was one of these Non-Conformist Puritans.

These devout Puritans were first given their name in the early 1560s as a term of derision. They were so labeled because of their efforts to purify the Church of England according to the standard of Scripture. Moreover, they sought to purify their personal lives in every area of their existence. The Puritans distinguished themselves by their unwavering loyalty to the supreme authority of Scripture. They insisted that the beliefs and practices of every believer and each church must yield to the high ground of biblical truth. As they followed in the footsteps of the Reformers, the Puritans became the new champions of *sola Scriptura*—Scripture alone.

John Bunyan was one of the most Bible-saturated Puritans of this period. The Prince of Preachers, Charles Spurgeon, aptly called Bunyan "a living Bible," describing him as one who bled out of every pore of his being "Bibline."[3] Bunyan was a prolific author, not only writing *The Pilgrim's Progress*, but penning many other Christian classics, including *Grace Abounding to the Chief of Sinners*. It should also be noted that the Bedford tinker was a preacher par excellence. In the pulpit, he was a force for God, unleashing the power of Scripture in his biblical expositions. Though he was untrained and unlettered, his preaching ministry was attended by supernatural unction from on high.

At first, the authorities were fairly tolerant of Bunyan, withholding his arrest and imprisonment. But Bunyan knew that being indicted for preaching without a government-approved license was imminent. Nevertheless, he preached. He was apprehended and taken to the county jail in Silver Street, Bedford, where he was held

3. H. J. Harrald, ed., *The Autobiography of Charles H. Spurgeon*, vol. 4, *1878–1892* (Philadelphia: American Baptist Publication Society, 1892), 268.

for most of twelve years. Afterward, Bunyan became pastor of the Bedford church, only to be arrested and taken into custody again for preaching without a license. Though he was imprisoned, the Word of God was not imprisoned with him, as he remained ever active in his writing and preaching ministry. Eager crowds gathered outside his jail cell to hear him expound the Scriptures. It was said by the renowned Puritan John Owen that he would give up all his impressive learning if he could preach like the tinker from Bedford.[4]

The evangelical church today stands in dire need of recapturing the influence of John Bunyan. In a day when many churches possess the mere façade of external religion, the story of Bunyan needs to be retold and his spirit recaptured. Here is one solitary individual who, though weak in himself, was mightily empowered when the church stood in great need of spiritual awakening. Despite the centuries that have since passed, Bunyan remains as relevant today as when he lived and served the Lord.

Joel Beeke and Paul Smalley are to be commended for giving us a compelling look into the spiritual life and gospel ministry of John Bunyan. They trace a golden thread through Bunyan's experience and teaching: *the fear of the Lord*. Few themes are as neglected today as the fear of God. Such fear is often viewed as psychologically harmful instead of as a delightful and energizing force for obedience. Bunyan stands as a preeminent example of the Puritan quest to find release from the guilty fear of God's wrath through the saving righteousness of Jesus Christ and to bow joyfully before God with a childlike fear. In their exposition of fear in Bunyan's life and doctrine, Beeke and Smalley open a window into the soul of true godliness—that reverent love for God's glory that is fed by the doctrines of God's sovereign grace.

Who better to introduce us to this stalwart Puritan than these two authors? Whether you are already familiar with this pivotal

4. See John Brown, *John Bunyan: His Life, Times, and Work* (London: Hulbert, 1928), 366.

figure or are simply desiring an initial introduction, you will want to devour and digest these pages. Properly researched and skillfully written, this volume will be a dose of strong medicine for the spiritual health of your soul.

Let me encourage you to read this book carefully. Be inspired by its story. Internalize its substance. Each one of us needs to personally experience the same depth of sanctifying work that God performed in this outstanding Christian leader, John Bunyan.

Steven J. Lawson
President, OnePassion Ministries
Dallas, Texas

Note on Abbreviations and Sources

Abbreviations

Luther, *Galatians*	Martin Luther, *A Commentarie of Master Doctor Martin Luther upon the Epistle of S. Paul to the Galathians* (London: George Miller, 1644).
ODNB	*Oxford Dictionary of National Biography* (Oxford: Oxford University Press, 2004).
Works	*The Works of John Bunyan*, ed. George Offor, 3 vols. (1854; repr., Edinburgh, UK: Banner of Truth, 1991).
Works (1692)	*The Works of that Eminent Servant of Christ Mr. John Bunyan, the First Volume* (London: William Marshall, 1692).

Sources

Seventeenth-century books may be viewed on Early English Books Online (EEBO). We have used the third edition of *The*

Pilgrim's Progress (1679) because it is the first one that contains the full story as we know it today. In citations of old sources, we have adjusted spelling to modern American standards, changed archaic grammatical forms such as verbs ending in –eth, and replaced the "thou" forms with "you" except in direct address to God or in Scripture quotations, but have otherwise left the words unchanged. Modern editions are cited alongside seventeenth-century books for ease of reference. Thus, beside each citation of Bunyan we also refer to the corresponding pages in the Offor edition of Bunyan's *Works*, reprinted by The Banner of Truth, as this is the most accessible edition today.

1

John Bunyan's Pilgrimage to Peace

John Bunyan (1628–1688) lived in fearful times.[1] Over the course of his six decades spanning the middle of the seventeenth century, England was visited by deadly plagues and torn apart by civil wars. The land seethed with social unrest; some even tried to bring in the kingdom of God by fomenting an uprising to overthrow the government. England's Stuart kings often tried to rule without Parliament, and one of these kings perished at the hands of the state. A historian remarks that Bunyan saw "the most turbulent, seditious, and factious sixty years of recorded English history."[2] Bunyan himself lost his first wife and spent more than twelve years in prison. His personal life was full of hardship, persecution, and suffering.

However, Bunyan was not a man who was shaken by current events or personal sorrows, but one who had learned "to live upon

1. For a summary of Bunyan's biography, see Richard L. Greaves, "Bunyan, John," in *ODNB,* 8:702–11. Portions of these first two chapters adapt some material from Joel R. Beeke and Randall J. Pederson, *Meet the Puritans* (Grand Rapids: Reformation Heritage Books, 2006), 101–12.

2. Christopher Hill, *A Tinker and a Poor Man: John Bunyan and His Church, 1628–1688* (New York: Alfred A. Knopf, 1989), 4.

God that is invisible" (see Heb. 11:27).[3] His endurance in faith and obedience to Jesus Christ prompted a recent biographer to give him the title of "Fearless Pilgrim."[4] Like Christian in his famous allegory, *The Pilgrim's Progress*, Bunyan persevered past all the spiritual lions and giants on his way to the Celestial City. Yet one writer has criticized Bunyan severely for his "fear-dominated theology."[5] Another writer wrote less critically, "If we single out the predominant tone of Bunyan's sermons, we would have to give priority to fear."[6] Which was he: fearless or fear-dominated? In reality, Bunyan believed that Christian courage and fear were inseparable. In many ways, he was like his own fictional character Mr. Godly-fear, whom he described as "a man of courage, conduct, and valour."[7]

Who was Bunyan? How could he be a man of such courage and yet of such great fear? To answer these questions, we must go back nearly four hundred years to a village in England.

The Beginnings of an Unlikely Pilgrim

John Bunyan was born in 1628 in the village of Elstow, near Bedford, to Thomas and Margaret (Bentley) Bunyan. John was baptized on November 30, 1628, in the local parish of the Church of England. It does not appear that his parents brought him up in the nurture and admonition of the Lord, for as a youth he scarcely knew how to talk without using profanity.[8]

At the time, King Charles I ruled Britain (r. 1625–1649). William Laud had risen to be bishop of London (later to become archbishop

3. John Bunyan, *Grace Abounding to the Chief of Sinners*, 8th ed. (London: Nath. Ponder, 1692), 164; see *Works*, 1:48.

4. Faith Cook, *Fearless Pilgrim: The Life and Times of John Bunyan* (Darlington, UK: Evangelical Press, 2008).

5. Alfred Noyes, quoted in *ODNB*, 8:710.

6. E. Beatrice Batson, "The Artistry of John Bunyan's Sermons," *Westminster Theological Journal* 38, no. 2 (Winter 1976): 180.

7. John Bunyan, *The Holy War, Made by Shaddai upon Diabolus . . . Or, the Losing and Taking Again of the Town of Mansoul* (London: Nat. Ponder, 1696), 283; see *Works*, 3:351.

8. Bunyan, *Grace Abounding*, 13; see *Works*, 1:9.

of Canterbury), and those holding to Reformed doctrine and piety found themselves in ever-increasing disfavor in church and state as a result of the rise of Laud's high-church Arminian party. In 1620, the Separatists of the "Pilgrim Fathers" had sailed for the New World, and in 1630, John Winthrop led the beginnings of a major Puritan exodus to New England.

Bunyan's family, however, living in a village more than fifty miles north of London, may have felt removed from such political and ecclesiastical conflicts. Though their ancestors in the sixteenth century had been landowners in the manor of Elstow, declining fortunes had left them relatively poor. His father was a tinker—a brazier or tinsmith who repaired vessels made of soft metal, such as cooking pots and pans. Bunyan learned to read and write but otherwise was not well educated.

Bunyan soon displayed the evils of his sinful heart. He later wrote, "It was my delight to be taken captive by the devil at his will (2 Tim. 2:26), being filled with all unrighteousness . . . from a child that I had but few equals . . . both for cursing, swearing, lying, and blaspheming the holy name of God."[9] That is not to say that he had nothing to rebuke or restrain his run into ungodliness. Death was always near in the seventeenth century—in 1636, the plague visited England again, killing thirty thousand people or more. When he was nine or ten years old, nightmares and spasms of conscience frightened him and made him wish that there was no such thing as hell, but he quickly cast off these fleeting religious impressions. He became "the very ringleader of all the youth that kept me company in all manner of vice and ungodliness."[10]

In 1642, the kingdom was plunged into turmoil when conflict between King Charles I and Parliament erupted into civil war.

9. Bunyan, *Grace Abounding*, 2–3; see *Works*, 1:6.
10. Bunyan, *Grace Abounding*, 4; see *Works*, 1:6–7.

Tragedy also struck at Bunyan's home. At age sixteen, he experienced "shock and misery," for his mother and sister died a month apart.[11] His father quickly remarried. John joined the Parliamentary forces in 1644, later organized as the New Model Army under Oliver Cromwell. He served in the garrison at Newport Pagnell, a unit that was "chronically behind in its pay and poorly equipped."[12]

On one occasion, God spared his life in a remarkable manner: "When I was a soldier, I, with others, were drawn out to go to such a place to besiege it; but when I was just ready to go, one of the company desired to go in my room; to which when I consented, he took my place; and coming to the siege, as he stood sentinel, he was shot into the head with a musket bullet, and died."[13]

He may have heard the gospel preached by Puritans and the more radical sectarians among soldiers. It is also possible that Bunyan had been exposed to Baptist teachings as early as 1642, when Benjamin Coxe was preaching in Bedford. Coxe was later a signatory of the 1644 London Confession of Faith, an early Particular Baptist confession.[14]

Civil war would break out again in 1648, but, in 1647, Bunyan left the army and returned to the life of a tinker. His portable stake anvil was discovered in 1905 with his name and the year 1647 inscribed on it. Like the pilgrim of whom he wrote, he understood what it meant to carry a burden; the anvil weighs sixty pounds.

In January 1649, Charles I was put on trial, condemned, and executed as a traitor. England suspended its monarchy and became a commonwealth. That same year, Bunyan married; we do not know his bride's name. Further trials arrived for the new family when

11. Jay Green, "Bunyan, John," in *The Encyclopedia of Christianity*, ed. Gary G. Cohen (Marshalltown, DE: The National Foundation for Christian Education, 1968), 2:221.

12. *ODNB*, 8:702.

13. Bunyan, *Grace Abounding*, 6; see *Works*, 1:7.

14. Richard L. Greaves, *Glimpses of Glory: John Bunyan and English Dissent* (Stanford, CA: Stanford University Press, 2002), 62; Joseph Ivimey, *A History of the English Baptists*, vol. 2 (London: for the author, 1814), 14.

their first child, Mary, baptized on July 20, 1650, was born blind.[15] Three more children would follow.

Here, then, we have a young man in his early twenties with a history of irreverence and rebellion. He had suffered the death of mother and sister and had seen the horrors of war while yet a teenager. He was a man with little education who worked with his hands—a "mechanic," in the language of his day. He might have lived and died in obscurity, with a dirty mouth and a dirty soul. For such a man to become a godly Christian pastor seems unlikely, and to become a premier Christian author seems almost impossible. There is a powerful lesson for us in the early life of Bunyan. The apostle Paul expresses it in 1 Corinthians 1:26–27: "Ye see your calling, brethren, how that not many wise men after the flesh, not many mighty, not many noble, are called: but God hath chosen the foolish things of the world to confound the wise." John Bunyan is a shining example of God's sovereign freedom to choose whom He pleases. One of the first steps in the fear of the Lord is recognizing that God is God and that we are not.

The Lord delights to turn human expectations upside down. He does this for a noble purpose: "that no flesh should glory in his presence" (1 Cor. 1:29). Instead, Christ is everything to believers—"wisdom, and righteousness, and sanctification, and redemption: that, according as it is written, He that glorieth, let him glory in the Lord" (vv. 30–31). If you have faith in Christ and love for His people, then give thanks to God (see Eph. 1:15–16). If you have gifts and abilities, do not boast in yourself, but boast in the Lord, for your talents are the gracious gifts of Christ (see Eph. 4:7). Furthermore, as we look at other people, let us judge no man according to the flesh (see 2 Cor. 5:16). God can take anyone, even the chief of sinners, and make that person into a useful servant of Jesus Christ. Yes, even if you have cursed God all your life and seen tragedy and

15. Hill, *A Tinker and a Poor Man*, 57, 59.

violence, God can make something beautiful of your life through Jesus Christ. But it must begin in the heart, as it did with Bunyan.

The Work of God in the Heart

Bunyan's godly wife came from a poor family, but she brought him a dowry of two books. One was *The Plain Man's Pathway to Heaven* by Arthur Dent (1553–1607), a devotional classic that presents the gospel and Christian life through a conversation shared by four men. The other was *The Practice of Piety* by Lewis Bayly (c. 1575–1631), another classic describing God, heaven, hell, and the cultivation of piety as a way to prepare for Christ's return. Bunyan and his wife sometimes read these books together, and she told him about the holy lifestyle of her father.

Bunyan responded to these Christian influences with an outward show of religion and superstitious regard for the priests and ceremonies of the Church of England. His pastor, Christopher Hall, preached a strong sermon against breaking the Sabbath, but Bunyan ignored it and played his usual games on the Lord's Day. However, his conscience struck him, and he began to wonder if he was damned beyond all hope. This despair hardened him further, and he "went on to sin with great greediness of mind," until a woman, herself with a very poor reputation, rebuked him for swearing and cursing so much that she feared he would corrupt all the youth of the town. This rebuke so shamed Bunyan that he broke off his habit of perpetual swearing. He also began to read his Bible and reform his morals with an outward keeping of God's commandments, yet he remained ignorant of Jesus Christ and His saving work.[16]

This was a time of Puritan ascendancy in England. At the Battle of Worcester (Sept. 3, 1651), Oliver Cromwell led the New Model Army to defeat Royalist forces, causing Charles II, son of the executed monarch, to flee England for France. From 1653 to 1658,

16. Bunyan, *Grace Abounding*, 10–14; see *Works*, 1:8–9.

Cromwell ruled England as the lord protector. This decade was a period of multiplication of religious sects of many kinds. However, it was also a time when the Puritans, committed to Reformed evangelical truth and godliness, could gather in freedom and worship God according to their consciences. Bunyan would meet such people, and by their example and witness God changed his life.

One day, Bunyan's work as a tinker took him to Bedford, and he came across "three or four poor women sitting at a door, in the sun, talking about the things of God." Considering himself quite a religious man by now, he went to talk with them. However, what he heard shook him.

> I heard, but I understood not; for they were far above, out of my reach: their talk was about a new birth, the work of God on their hearts, also how they were convinced of their miserable state by nature; they talked how God had visited their souls with his love in the Lord Jesus, and with what words and promises they had been refreshed, comforted and supported against the temptation of the devil.... They also discoursed of their own wretchedness of heart, their unbelief; and did contemn, slight and abhor [despise and hate] their own righteousness, as filthy and insufficient to do them any good. And I thought they spoke, as if joy did make them speak.[17]

He simultaneously found his hypocrisy exposed and a desire stirred in his heart to have what these women possessed. They introduced him to their pastor, John Gifford, who led the Independent (Congregational) church in Bedford. Gifford had been a major in the king's army and then an apothecary or pharmacist in Bedford, living an immoral life until his conversion through reading a book by the Puritan Robert Bolton (1572–1631). The church was organized in 1650

17. Bunyan, *Grace Abounding*, 17; see *Works*, 1:10. The original says, "me-thought they spake."

and chose Gifford, one of the founding members, as their pastor. In 1653, he also was appointed the rector of the parish of St. John the Baptist in Bedford, where he served until his death on September 21, 1655. The qualifications for membership in the Independent congregation consisted simply of "faith in Christ and holiness of life."[18] Gifford invited Bunyan to his home to hear discussions "about the dealings of God with the soul," which deepened his convictions of sin.[19]

Bunyan entered into a season of great questioning and searching that lasted perhaps as late as 1658.[20] He encountered the Ranters, a pantheistic, antinomian movement associated with sexual immorality and social upheaval, but he rejected their radical teachings.[21] Far more significant for Bunyan were his intense struggles with doubt, guilt, fear, despair, and temptations to blaspheme God. The Bible alternately terrified him with divine wrath and offered him divine grace in what has been called "the battle of the texts" within Bunyan's mind.[22] During this time, he found comfort in his growing understanding of the death of the incarnate Lord Jesus to satisfy God's justice and give sinners peace with God (see 2 Cor. 5:21; Col. 1:20; Heb. 2:14–15). He received much help from "the ministry of holy Mr. Gifford, whose doctrine, by God's grace, was much for my stability."[23]

Bunyan was also blessed by reading the commentary of Martin Luther (1483–1546) on the epistle to the Galatians, in which he found his own experience "largely and profoundly handled, as if his book had been written out of my own heart."[24] Luther's commentary (1535)

18. Quoted in Greaves, *Glimpses of Glory*, 63. On Gifford, see J. S. Macauley, "Gifford, John," in *Biographical Dictionary of British Radicals in the Seventeenth Century*, ed. Richard L. Greaves and Robert Zaller (Brighton, UK: Harvester, 1983), 2:9.

19. Bunyan, *Grace Abounding*, 36–37; see *Works*, 1:15.

20. *ODNB*, 8:702.

21. On the complexities of understanding the Ranters, see Greaves, *Glimpses of Glory*, 67–74.

22. Hill, *A Tinker and a Poor Man*, 66–68.

23. Bunyan, *Grace Abounding*, 56; see *Works*, 1:20.

24. Richard L. Greaves, *John Bunyan*, Courtenay Studies in Reformation Theology 2 (Grand Rapids: Eerdmans, 1969), 18.

was first translated from Latin into English in 1575 and reprinted at least seven more times through 1644, showing its popularity in Britain. Its editor addressed the opening epistle, "To all afflicted consciences which groan for salvation."[25] Luther taught that "the true way to Christianity" is to acknowledge yourself to be a sinner for whom it is impossible to do any good work commanded by the law, and, instead of seeking salvation by works, to trust that God sent His only begotten Son to die for sinners and give them life.[26] Bunyan's experience would have resonated deeply with Luther's words: "God must therefore have a strong hammer, or a mighty maul to break the rocks . . . that when a man by this bruising and breaking is brought to nothing, he should despair of his own strength, righteousness and holiness, and being thus thoroughly terrified, should thirst after mercy and remission of sins."[27] And Bunyan no doubt found hope in statements like this: "Faith takes hold of Christ, and has him present, and holds him enclosed, as the ring does the precious stone. And whosoever shall be found having this confidence in Christ apprehended in the heart, him will God account for righteous. . . . Wherefore God does accept or account us as righteous, only for our faith in Christ."[28]

The real breakthrough came when Bunyan grasped the truth that Christ's righteousness is imputed or credited by God to every believer. While Bunyan was walking through a field one day, God revealed Christ's righteousness to his soul and brought him to assurance. Bunyan wrote of that unforgettable experience,

> One day, as I was passing in the field . . . this sentence fell upon my soul: *Your Righteousness is in heaven*; and I thought withal, I saw with the eyes of my soul, Jesus Christ at God's right hand, there,

25. Luther, *Galatians*, A2r.
26. Luther, *Galatians*, fol. 62v–63r [on Gal. 2:16].
27. Luther, *Galatians*, fol. 166v [on Gal. 3:23].
28. Luther, *Galatians*, fol. 65v–66r [on Gal. 2:16].

> I say, was my righteousness; so that wherever I was, or whatever I was a-doing, God could not say of me, "He wants [lacks] my righteousness," for that was just before Him. I also saw, moreover, that it was not my good frame of heart that made my righteousness better, nor yet my bad frame that made my righteousness worse; for my righteousness was Jesus Christ himself, "the same yesterday, today, and for ever" (Heb. 13:8). Now did my chains fall off my legs indeed, I was loosed from my afflictions and irons, my temptations also fled away. . . . Now I went also home rejoicing for the grace and love of God. . . . I lived, for some time, very sweetly at peace with God through Christ. O I thought Christ! Christ! There was nothing but Christ that was before my eyes.[29]

Bunyan found peace when he was enabled to look outside himself and rest his heart on Christ. With Christ as his righteousness, he need not fear the righteous judgment of God. As Luther wrote, "Therefore when the law accuses and sin terrifies him, he looks upon Christ, and when he has apprehended him by faith, he has present with him the Conqueror of the law, sin, death, and the devil: who reigns and rules over them, so that they cannot hurt him."[30]

The tinker of Bedford would face tremendous trials in his Christian pilgrimage. At times, he struggled with depression. Yet he persistently demonstrated remarkable spiritual strength, courage, and endurance. As one forgiven of his wickedness and declared righteous by God, he was enabled to live out Proverbs 28:1: "The wicked flee when no man pursueth: but the righteous are bold as a lion." God dug deep into his heart to lay a rock-solid foundation that would endure much tribulation in days to come.

We need lions for the Lord today—not men and women who bite and devour each other in self-righteous hatred, but people

29. Bunyan, *Grace Abounding*, 116–18; see *Works*, 1:35–36.
30. Luther, *Galatians*, fol. 66v [on Gal. 2:16].

humbled by God's law and made strong by Christ's righteousness. We need people who can stand up for righteousness before the rich men and judges of this world because they know that they are counted as righteous by the Judge of all the earth. Before you can serve the Lord, you must be saved by the Lord.

2

Preacher and Prisoner for Christ

Even while John Bunyan wrestled Jacob-like with God until he knew His blessing, the tinker found himself drawn into ministry. Bunyan's fear of the Lord was productive; it did not lead him into a sterile passivity but energized him to work for the cause of truth, meekness, and righteousness. In fact, Bunyan would endure remarkable sufferings as a preacher and teacher of the Word, but he overcame them all to influence not just England but people all over the world. God's remarkable providence took a commoner from an English village and used his ministry to bless millions to this very day.

His life reminds us of the words of another unlikely convert, the apostle Paul: "By the grace of God I am what I am: and his grace which was bestowed upon me was not in vain; but I laboured more abundantly than they all: yet not I, but the grace of God which was with me" (1 Cor. 15:10). Paul's experience of grace put a new kind of fear within him that proved to be a driving engine of his service to the Lord. He said, "For we must all appear before the judgment seat of Christ; that every one may receive the things done in his body, according to that he hath done, whether it be good or bad. Knowing therefore the terror of the Lord, we persuade men" (2 Cor. 5:10–11). In the same way, Bunyan's deliverance from the craven fear of damnation was also his entrance into a holy and loving fear of God that moved him to preach the truth of Christ no matter how men opposed him.

Engaged with Voice and Pen for the Kingdom

After John Gifford, Bunyan's pastor, died in 1655, he was replaced by John Burton. Bunyan was called upon increasingly by the Bedford church to preach, though he had not yet fully emerged from the darkness of his spiritual depression into the sunshine of assurance of faith. In addition to preaching, he published his first book, *Some Gospel-Truths Opened* (1656), and a *Vindication* (1657) of the former, after clashing with the Society of Friends, or Quakers.[1]

In an "Epistle to the Reader" in *Some Gospel-Truths*, Burton commended Bunyan as a man "not chosen out of an earthly, but out of the heavenly university, the church of Christ," who "has not the learning or wisdom of man, yet, through grace, he has received the teaching of God." Already the "saints" had experience of Bunyan's "soundness in the faith, of his godly conversation, and his ability to preach . . . with much success in the conversion of sinners."[2] He had quickly risen in the estimation of the Bedford church as a Christian and a preacher. He also attracted the hostile attention of the authorities, being indicted for illegal ("unlicensed") preaching in the village of Eaton Socon, Bedfordshire, perhaps in early 1658—though without serious consequences. He preached the next year in the parish church of Yelden at the request of the rector, William Dell, provoking thirty of Dell's parishioners to seek his removal as rector.[3]

1. John Bunyan, *Grace Abounding to the Chief of Sinners*, 8th ed. (London: Nath. Ponder, 1692), 60; see *Works*, 1:21. It should be noted that the teachings of the Friends has changed since the mid-seventeenth century, and some modern Quakers embrace many evangelical beliefs.

2. John Burton, "To the Reader," in John Bunyan, *Some Gospel-Truths Opened* (London: J. Wright, 1656), A10v–A12r; see *Works*, 2:141.

3. *ODNB*, 8:703–4.

Storm clouds were gathering for the Nonconformists. Social unrest continued among religious radicals. Thomas Venner had organized his Fifth Monarchist followers, gathered horses and weapons, and printed a theocratic manifesto to establish the kingdom of the saints on earth, when, in 1657, the government arrested and imprisoned him before the uprising could begin.[4] The following year, Lord Protector Oliver Cromwell died, leaving England in the less capable hands of his son Richard. Bunyan at this time published *A Few Sighs from Hell*, an exposition of Luke 16:19–31, the parable of the rich man ("Dives") and Lazarus. The book attacks professional clergy and the wealthy who promote carnality. It was well received and helped to establish Bunyan as a reputable writer. About that same time, his wife passed away, leaving him alone with their young children.

In 1659, Bunyan published *The Doctrine of the Law and Grace Unfolded*, which expounds his view of covenant theology, stressing the promissory nature of the covenant of grace and the dichotomy between law and grace. This helped to establish him as a theologian holding to the Reformed doctrine of salvation, though it led to false charges of antinomianism by Richard Baxter.

Thomas Smith (1624–1661), a Cambridge librarian described as "a learned and pugnacious man," attacked Bunyan in 1659 for not being competent or authorized to preach, being a mere tinker.[5] This prompted General Baptist Henry Denne (d. 1661) to reply, "You seem angry with the tinker because he strives to mend souls as well as kettles and pans," while pointing out that Bunyan was duly commissioned by the church in Bedford.[6] Smith's reply, citing

4. Richard L. Greaves, *Glimpses of Glory: John Bunyan and English Dissent* (Stanford, CA: Stanford University Press, 2002), 90.

5. Thomas Smith, *The Quaker Disarm'd, or A True Relation of a Late Public Dispute Held at Cambridge . . . With A Letter in Defence of the Ministry, and against Lay-Preachers* (London: J. C., 1659). On Thomas Smith, see John Peile, *Biographical Register of Christ's College* (Cambridge: Cambridge University Press, 1910), 1:468.

6. Henry Denne, *The Quaker no Papist, in Answer to The Quaker Disarmed* (London: Francis Smith, 1659), A2r. On Denne, see B. R. White, "Denne, Henry," in *Biographical*

Bunyan's book, accused the tinker of antinomianism because he said that sinners should "come to Christ," yes, "even as filthy as ever you can."[7] He took this as an encouragement to sin. However, Smith had confused the free offer of the gospel of justification by faith alone with antinomianism. The context of Bunyan's statement is as follows:

> [Objector's] *Reply.* All this we confess that Jesus Christ died for us: but he that thinks to be saved by Christ, and lives in his sins, shall never be saved.
>
> *Answer.* I grant that. But this I say again, a man must not make his good doings the lowest round of the ladder, by which he goes to heaven; that is, he that will, and shall go to heaven, must wholly, and alone, without any of his own things, venture his precious soul upon Jesus Christ and his merits.
>
> *Question.* What, and come to Christ as a sinner?
>
> *Answer.* Yea, with all your sins upon you, even as filthy as ever you can.[8]

Bunyan anticipated the objection that if Christ has fully satisfied God's justice, then men may sin without fear. He answered it with the doctrine of union with Christ: "Rebel, rebel, there are some in Christ and some out of him; they that are in him have their sins forgiven, and they themselves made new creatures, and have the Spirit of the Son, which is a holy, loving, self-denying Spirit. . . .

Dictionary of British Radicals in the Seventeenth Century, ed. Richard L. Greaves and Robert Zaller (Brighton, UK: Harvester, 1983), 1:223.

7. Thomas Smith, *A Gagg for the Quakers, with an Answer to Mr. Denn's Quaker No Papist* (London: J. C., 1659), Ar.

8. John Bunyan, *The Doctrine of the Law and Grace Unfolded* (London: M. Wright, 1659), 297; see *Works,* 1:556.

The breathings of their souls is as much for sanctifying grace, as pardoning grace, that they might live a holy life."[9]

In this treatise, he also commended to his readers a book by John Dod and Robert Cleaver, *A Plain and Familiar Exposition of the Ten Commandments*[10]—a book that said of the Ten Commandments that "we must settle ourselves to obey them without resistance or gain-saying," for they were spoken by God and imprinted on the consciences of all mankind.[11] Bunyan was no antinomian, but he refused to confound justification by faith alone with sanctification unto good works; he wrote, "Obedience to the law is a fruit of our believing."[12] The law served both to thunder God's wrath against sinners and "as a rule, or directory" to those hidden in Christ, for they are "under the law to Christ" (1 Cor. 9:21).[13] In his posthumous publication, *Paul's Departure and Crown*, he warned against "those pleasant songs and music that gospel sermons make where only grace is preached, and nothing of our duty," for Christ's disciples "have a work to do, even a work of self-denial."[14]

In 1659, Bunyan married a woman named Elizabeth, who took on the role of mother to the four children of his deceased first wife, including blind Mary. She proved to be a tremendous support to him and his children in the trials that lay ahead. In 1660, England restored Charles II to the monarchy, and the Anglican bishops returned to power in the national church. Despite the king's promises, the authorities began to persecute those who dissented from the Church of England. The Independent church in Bedford lost the privilege of using the building of St. John's but continued to meet elsewhere.

9. Bunyan, *The Doctrine of the Law and Grace Unfolded*, 289; see *Works*, 1:554.

10. Bunyan, *The Doctrine of the Law and Grace Unfolded*, 28 [margin]; see *Works*, 1:502.

11. John Dod and Robert Cleaver, *A Plaine and Familiar Exposition of the Ten Commaundements* (London: by Humfrey Lownes for Thomas Man, 1606), 2.

12. John Bunyan, *A Vindication of the Book Called, Some Gospel-Truths Opened* (London: Matthias Cowley, 1657), 15; see *Works*, 2:190.

13. John Bunyan, *Of the Law and a Christian*, in *Works* (1692), 191; see *Works*, 2:388.

14. John Bunyan, *Paul's Departure and Crown*, in *Works* (1692), 182; see *Works*, 1:734.

While some people may think of Bunyan merely as a storyteller, we have seen that his early ministry launched him into theological controversy. He loved the truth and fought for it with the weapons of loving persuasion. The fear of the Lord cannot leave us indifferent to the Word of God; when we fear Him, we sense the infinite weightiness of His Word. Truth becomes a matter of life and death. Proverbs 13:13–14 says,

> Whoso despiseth the word shall be destroyed: but he that feareth the commandment shall be rewarded.
> The law of the wise is a fountain of life, to depart from the snares of death.

It was this sense of God's glory in the Word that empowered Bunyan to keep preaching even when it cost him his freedom.

Imprisoned in the School of Faith

On November 12, 1660, Bunyan was arrested when he went to preach in the village of Lower Samsell, Bedfordshire. The authorities imprisoned him for failing to attend the services of the parish church, holding an illegal meeting or "conventicle," and preaching without a license from the Church of England. He said, "I should not leave speaking the Word of God: even to counsel, comfort, exhort, and teach the people."[15] The shock of his imprisonment sent his young wife into premature labor, and her baby died. Bunyan was offered release if he promised to stop preaching, but he insisted, "If I was out of prison today, I would preach the gospel again tomorrow, with the help of God."[16] His case was not helped when Venner led a violent Fifth Monarchy uprising in early 1661, terrorizing London and provoking even greater suspicion of

15. John Bunyan, *Relation of the Imprisonment of Mr. John Bunyan* (London: James Buckland, 1765), 8; see *Works*, 1:51.

16. Bunyan, *Relation of the Imprisonment*, 28; see *Works*, 1:57.

Nonconformists, including men such as John Owen (1616–1683) and Matthew Meade (1629–1699).[17]

In August 1661, at the Assizes—periodic county court sessions to hear both civil and criminal cases—Elizabeth Bunyan made a brave appeal for her husband. She was very young (perhaps nineteen or twenty) and had recently lost a child, but she stood up to these powerful men with amazing courage. She pleaded repeatedly for his release from prison, and at least one of the judges had some compassion for her, but the court rejected her plea. One justice told Bunyan's wife that he was "a pestilent fellow."

Another asked, "Will your husband leave off preaching? If he will do so, then send for him."

She replied, "My Lord, he dares not leave preaching, as long as he can speak." So they accused him of being a "breaker of the peace." But she said that he desired to live peacefully, to pursue his calling, and to provide for his family, including his four small children, one of whom was blind.

A justice said, "He will preach and do what he lists [as he pleases]."

His wife said, "He preaches nothing but the Word of God."

Another judge became so angry that she thought he was going to hit her. He told her that Bunyan preached the doctrine of the devil.

She replied, "My Lord, when the righteous Judge shall appear, it will be known that his doctrine is not the doctrine of the devil."[18] John Brown later commented, "Elizabeth Bunyan was simply an English peasant woman: could she have spoken with more dignity had she been a crowned queen?"[19]

So Bunyan went to prison because he refused to give up preaching the gospel and would not worship with the Church of England. He would remain in prison for twelve years.

17. Christopher Hill, *A Tinker and a Poor Man: John Bunyan and His Church, 1628–1688* (New York: Alfred A. Knopf, 1989), 138–39.

18. Bunyan, *Relation of the Imprisonment*, 44–46; see *Works*, 1:61.

19. John Brown, *John Bunyan: His Life, Times, and Work* (London: Hulbert, 1928), 150.

These were dark days in England. On August 24, 1662, under the latest Act of Uniformity, some two thousand ministers were ejected from their pulpits because they would not submit to ordination by bishops or conform to the liturgy of the Book of Common Prayer. The Conventicle Acts (1664) prohibited unauthorized gatherings for public worship. The Five Mile Act (1665) forbade Nonconformist ministers from coming within five miles of the place of their former ministry or any incorporated town. The bubonic plague swept through London in 1665, killing more than a hundred thousand people and compelling the king and many of the rich to vacate the city. When the plague began to subside, the Great Fire of London engulfed the city in early September 1666, destroying thousands of buildings and leaving many homeless and destitute.

Bunyan suffered greatly in prison. We catch a glimpse of his experience from the account in *The Pilgrim's Progress* when Giant Despair throws Christian and Faithful "into a very dark dungeon, nasty and stinking."[20] Bunyan especially felt the pain of separation from his wife and children, describing it as a "pulling of the flesh from my bones," and when he thought of his blind daughter unprotected, cold, and begging for food, he felt that it "would break my heart to pieces."[21] At times, he grew very depressed. Regarding an occasion early in his prison time, Bunyan wrote: "I was once above all the rest in a very sad and low condition for many weeks. . . . For indeed at that time all the things of God were hid from my soul."[22]

But God turned the Bedford jail into a school of faith. Here Bunyan learned "to live upon God that is invisible,"[23] entering experientially into the reality described by Paul in 2 Corinthians 4:18, "We look not at the things which are seen, but at the things which

20. John Bunyan, *The Pilgrim's Progress from This World, to That Which Is to Come*, 3rd ed. (London: Nath. Ponder, 1679), 195; see *Works*, 3:140.

21. Bunyan, *Grace Abounding*, 165; see *Works*, 1:48.

22. Bunyan, *Grace Abounding*, 169; see *Works*, 1:49.

23. Bunyan, *Grace Abounding*, 164; see *Works*, 1:48.

are not seen: for the things which are seen are temporal; but the things which are not seen are eternal."

The jailers occasionally permitted Bunyan limited freedom to leave the prison and preach. George Offor notes, "It is said that many of the Baptist congregations in Bedfordshire owe their origins to his midnight preaching."[24] He also preached to those with him in prison. One Lord's Day in jail, it was Bunyan's turn to preach to his fellow prisoners, but he found himself to be "empty, spiritless, and barren." However, looking through his Bible, he came upon the description of the heavenly Jerusalem at the end of the book of Revelation. His soul was dazzled by the splendor of God among His heavenly people. He took up the text with prayer, and he preached it with such power that he later enlarged it into a book, *The Holy City: or the New Jerusalem* (1665).[25]

Prison became the seedbed for Bunyan's greatest writings. In the mid-1660s, Bunyan wrote extensively with the Bible and Foxe's *Book of Martyrs* at his side. He composed *Profitable Meditations* in 1661, using poetry to declare God's sovereignty and man's responsibility to repent.[26] In 1663, he wrote *Prison Meditations* and *Christian Behaviour*, the latter intended as a handbook for Christian living and as a response against charges of antinomianism, as well as a last will and testament, since Bunyan expected to die soon in prison. He also finished *I Will Pray with the Spirit*, an exposition of 1 Corinthians 14:15, focused on the Spirit's inner work in all true prayer. Around this time, he also wrote a "broadside" (a single, large sheet of paper) about the working out of divine election and reprobation in people's lives, titled *A Map Showing the Order and Causes of Salvation*, which shows that he was familiar with a similar diagram found in the famous treatise on predestination by William

24. George Offor, "Memoir of John Bunyan," in *Works*, 1:lix.

25. John Bunyan, "The Epistle to the Readers," in *The Holy City: or the New Jerusalem* (London: J. Dover, 1665), A3r; see *Works*, 3:397.

26. *ODNB*, 8:704.

Perkins (1558–1602) titled *A Golden Chaine.*[27] In 1665, he published *One Thing Needful* and *The Resurrection of the Dead.* This latter work is a sequel to *The Holy City,* in which Bunyan expounded the resurrection from Acts 24:14–15 in a traditional way and then used his prison torments to illustrate the horrors that await the damned after the final judgment.

Bunyan also published his spiritual autobiography, *Grace Abounding to the Chief of Sinners* (1666), which details the struggles of his conversion and calling into the ministry. It went through six editions in his lifetime.[28] During the last part of his imprisonment, he finished *A Confession of My Faith, A Reason for My Practice,* and *A Defence of the Doctrine of Justification,* an uncompromising critique of the rising tide of Pelagianism among the Nonconformists and latitudinarianism among the Anglican establishment. In the preface to *A Confession of My Faith,* he declared, "I have determined the Almighty God being my help, and shield, yet to suffer, if frail life might continue so long, even till the moss shall grow on mine eyebrows, rather than violate my faith and principles."[29]

In 1670, Bunyan was joined in prison by Nehemiah Coxe, another preacher raised up within the Bedford congregation. Coxe remained in prison with Bunyan for at least a year.[30] Coxe went on to serve as one of the pastors at the Particular Baptist church in Petty, France, and appears to have played a key role in preparing the Second London Confession of 1677, reaffirmed by the Particular Baptists in 1689.[31] However, Bunyan did not see eye-to-eye with his fellow Baptists on all issues, as is evident in *A Confession*

27. Greaves, *Glimpses of Glory,* 173. The broadside was reprinted with the *Works* of 1692.

28. *ODNB,* 8:705.

29. John Bunyan, "To the Reader," in *A Confession of My Faith, and A Reason of My Practice* (London: Francis Smith, 1672), A6v; see *Works,* 2:594.

30. Greaves, *Glimpses of Glory,* 269.

31. Michael A. G. Haykin, *Kiffin, Knollys, and Keach: Rediscovering Our English Baptist Heritage* (Leeds, UK: Reformation Trust Today, 1996), 68–69. On Coxe, see Joseph Ivimey, *A History of the English Baptists,* vol. 2 (London: for the author, 1814), 403–7.

of My Faith, which "established Bunyan as an open-membership, open-communion Baptist with Reformed predestinarian views." This work provoked controversy with some Particular Baptists on the one hand—who adhered to "closed communion," refusing the sacrament to those who were not baptized as believers—and with General Baptists on the other—who rejected the Reformed view of salvation by sovereign grace alone.[32]

In 1672, Charles II issued the Royal Declaration of Indulgence. Bunyan was released from prison in May after twelve years of incarceration. The Bedford congregation, sensing some relaxation of the law against preaching, had already appointed Bunyan as their pastor on January 21, 1672. However, Parliament and the Church of England worked together to limit the freedoms granted in this indulgence by adopting measures such as the Test Act of 1672, which required anyone holding public office to take communion in the Church of England and to reject the Roman Catholic doctrine of transubstantiation (thus excluding Nonconformist Protestants and Roman Catholics). During this time, Bunyan wrote *Instruction for the Ignorant* (1675), a catechism for the saved and unsaved that emphasizes the need for self-denial; *Light for Them that Sit in Darkness* (1675), a polemical work against those who oppose atonement by Christ's satisfaction and justification by His imputed righteousness, especially the Quakers and Latitudinarians; *Saved by Grace* (1676), an exposition of Ephesians 2:5 that encourages the godly to persevere in the faith notwithstanding persecution; and *The Strait Gate* (1676), an exposition of Luke 13:24 that seeks to awaken sinners to the gospel message.

A warrant for Bunyan's arrest was issued on March 4, 1675, on the charge of preaching to a conventicle. He was imprisoned again from December 1676 to June 1677. Thomas Barlow, bishop of Lincoln, ordered the release of Bunyan upon a cautionary bond, dated June

32. *ODNB*, 8:706.

21, 1677. This took place after John Owen, an Independent minister, had interceded on Bunyan's behalf with Barlow and Heneage Finch, the Lord Chancellor.[33] Owen, a preeminent Reformed theologian who had served as vice-chancellor of Oxford University during the Protectorate, evidently admired the ministry of Bunyan. John Brown wrote that Owen told "King Charles that he would willingly exchange his learning for the tinker's power of touching men's hearts."[34]

Bunyan's life is an amazing paradox. On the one hand, his sermons and writings were powerful and widely disseminated. On the other hand, he was weak and long confined in the darkness of his prison. At times, that darkness seemed to overwhelm his soul. Yet his reverence and faith toward the Lord sustained him because he knew his God. Isaiah 50:10 says, "Who is among you that feareth the LORD, that obeyeth the voice of his servant, that walketh in darkness, and hath no light? Let him trust in the name of the LORD, and stay upon his God." Those who fear the Lord may pass through valleys of deep darkness, even through the shadow of death, but the Lord sustains them with such power that their very struggles to believe become mighty victories over the powers of darkness, and they become shining beacons to guide others toward heaven.

The Pilgrim's Progress to the Celestial City

During this latter period of imprisonment, Bunyan completed the first part of his famous *Pilgrim's Progress*, published in 1678 and a year later expanded in its third edition to the full story as we have it today. It may be that Owen encouraged Bunyan to put it into print and introduced him to his publisher, Nathaniel Ponder.[35]

The book tells an allegorical tale of the travels of pilgrims from the City of Destruction to the Celestial City. Richard Greaves calls it "an epic that creatively combined warfaring and wayfaring," for

33. Greaves, *Glimpses of Glory*, 344.
34. John Brown, *John Bunyan*, 366.
35. Greaves, *Glimpses of Glory*, 347.

"Christian is both pilgrim and warrior."[36] Like the "chapbooks" popular among the poor of Bunyan's day, it involves many adventures and conflicts with fiends, monsters, and giants. It relies upon dialogue among the travelers to communicate spiritual lessons about the Christian life, a method that Bunyan encountered in Arthur Dent's *The Plain Man's Pathway to Heaven*. It also uses symbolic characters with evocative names like Mr. Worldly-Wiseman, a feature that Bunyan may have learned from *The Isle of Man* (1627) by the Puritan Richard Bernard.[37] Moral allegories of this kind were common in English sermons from the medieval period onward.[38] Bunyan took up these literary tools in his tinker hands and crafted a brilliant and delightful story that opens up the Puritan doctrines of conversion, sanctification, and perseverance in a memorable and illuminating fashion.

The Pilgrim's Progress sold very well, though it would have cost the equivalent of a full day's wage for the working class—significantly more than the small chapbooks. One bookseller ordered 9,500 copies in 1690, and another bookseller 10,000 in 1692.[39] Charles Doe stated in 1692 that it had sold "about a hundred thousand in England," but how he calculated this number we cannot know.[40] A modern scholar estimated its seventeenth-century printings at "over 30,000 copies."[41] The book appeared in twenty-two editions by 1700, seventy editions by 1800, and more than thirteen hundred editions by the early twentieth century.[42] By 1682, it had been translated into Dutch

36. *ODNB*, 8:705.

37. W. R. Owens, "The Reception of *The Pilgrim's Progress* in England," in *Bunyan in England and Abroad*, ed. M. Van Os and G. J. Schutte (Amsterdam: VU University Press, 1990), 96; Hill, *A Tinker and a Poor Man*, 161, 165.

38. For suggestive parallels between the spiritual allegories of medieval sermons and Bunyan's stories, see Gerald R. Owst, *Literature and Pulpit in Medieval England* (Cambridge: Cambridge University Press, 1933), 97–109.

39. Owens, "The Reception of *The Pilgrim's Progress* in England," 92, 97.

40. Charles Doe, "The Struggler," in *Works* (1692), Ttttt2v.

41. N. H. Keeble, *The Literary Culture of Nonconformity in Later Seventeenth-Century England* (Leicester, UK: Leicester University Press, 1987), 128.

42. Greaves, *Glimpses of Glory*, 612.

and went through five Dutch editions in five years.[43] It was also translated into French and Welsh during Bunyan's lifetime. It has since been translated into more than two hundred languages and is one of the bestselling books of all time.[44]

Bunyan spent his last years ministering to the Nonconformists and writing. In 1678, he also published *Come, and Welcome, to Jesus Christ*, a popular exposition of John 6:37 that movingly proclaims the free offer of grace to sinners who flee to Jesus Christ to be saved, while teaching that all who come to Christ do so under the powerful influence of the electing Savior. This book went through six editions in the last decade of Bunyan's life. He published his *Treatise of the Fear of God* in 1679, a systematic examination of divine fear in both its negative and positive aspects. He wrote that the fear of the Lord is "the salt that seasons every duty," explaining, "For there is no duty performed by us, that can by any means be accepted of God, if it be not seasoned with godly fear."[45]

In 1680, he wrote *The Life and Death of Mr. Badman*, which has been described as "a series of snapshots depicting common attitudes and practices of the day against which Bunyan regularly preached."[46] Two years later, he published *The Greatness of the Soul* and *The Holy War.* In 1684, he published the second part of *The Pilgrim's Progress,* dealing with Christiana's pilgrimage, and in 1685, *A Caution to Stir Up to Watch against Sin*, and *Questions about the Nature and the Perpetuity of the Seventh-day Sabbath.*

The open door that released Bunyan from prison proved to be a gateway for the preaching of the gospel. Charles Doe, writing in 1692, recollected,

43. Jacques B. H. Alblas, "The Reception of *The Pilgrim's Progress* in Holland During the Eighteenth and Nineteenth Centuries," in *Bunyan in England and Abroad*, 121.

44. *ODNB*, 8:711.

45. John Bunyan, *A Treatise of the Fear of God* (London: N. Ponder, 1679), 2; see *Works*, 1:438.

46. *ODNB*, 8:707.

> And being out [of prison], he preached the gospel publicly at Bedford, and about the countries, and at London, with very great success, being mightily followed everywhere. And it pleased the Lord to preserve him out of the hands of his enemies in the severe persecution at the latter end of King Charles II's reign, though they often searched and laid wait for him, and sometimes narrowly missed him.[47]

Doe estimated that Bunyan preached to twelve hundred people at seven o'clock in the morning one weekday in the winter in London, and to three thousand on a Lord's Day.[48]

In 1685, Charles II died after being received into the Roman Catholic Church, and his Roman Catholic brother, James II, became king. King James sought to circumvent England's legal and social obstacles to his religion, such as the Test Acts. The nation was increasingly fearful of a return to the Roman Catholic religion, prompting a failed revolution by the Duke of Monmouth. In the tension of the times, Bunyan signed a deed of gift on December 23, 1685, to transfer the rights to all his possessions to his wife, anticipating a possible return to prison or worse. However, from the summer of 1686, James II "embraced a policy of toleration."[49] In 1687, an agent of the king reported that he had interviewed the "Pastor to the Dissenting Congregation" in Bedford, and Bunyan had declared his support "for electing only such members of Parliament as will certainly vote for repealing all the Tests and penal-Laws touching Religion."[50] Evidently Bunyan treasured liberty of conscience, even though it would also open a door for Roman Catholicism in England, a religion that Bunyan strongly opposed as Babylon and Antichrist.

47. Doe, "The Struggler," in Bunyan, *Works* (1692), Ttttt2r.
48. Doe, "The Struggler," in Bunyan, *Works* (1692), Ttttt2v.
49. *ODNB*, 8:708.
50. George Duckett, ed., *Penal Laws and Test Act: Questions Touching Their Repeal Propounded in 1687–8 by James II* (London, 1883), 59, available online at https://archive.org/details/penallawsandtes00firgoog.

In the last three years of his life, Bunyan continued his prolific output of godly literature. He wrote ten more books, including *The Pharisee and the Publican*, *The Jerusalem Sinner Saved*, and *The Work of Jesus Christ as an Advocate*. Throughout his life, he maintained a rigorous discipline of writing. Greaves estimates that Bunyan generated more than a thousand words a day in writing one theological treatise and may have averaged more than four hundred words a day, five days a week, for ten months, in writing *The Holy War*.[51] And he did all this in an age without computers, writing by hand, often in jail. His self-discipline is a marvel of God's grace.

In the summer of 1688, a man approached Bunyan seeking his help to reconcile the man to his estranged father. The Bedford pastor traveled to Reading and helped the family to make peace. On the way, Bunyan was drenched by a storm, and he developed a violent fever that appears to have been influenza, perhaps complicated by pneumonia. He died on August 31, 1688. The following Wednesday, the church in Bedford devoted itself to "prayer and humiliation for this heavy stroke upon us, the death of dear Brother Bunyan."[52] He was buried in Bunhill Fields, London, close to Thomas Goodwin and John Owen. His wife Elizabeth survived him by three years, dying in 1691. He was also survived by his sons John, Thomas, and Joseph, and by his daughters Elizabeth and Sarah (blind Mary had already died). His estate was valued at 42 pounds, 19 shillings. Either he received little by way of royalties for his many books, or he had given most of it away.[53]

Just a few months after Bunyan's death, the Glorious Revolution took place. Parliament overthrew James II and installed the Protestant William III and Mary II as king and queen. The Act of

51. Greaves, *Glimpses of Glory*, 603.

52. Richard L. Greaves, introduction to *The Miscellaneous Works of John Bunyan*, vol. 11, *Good News for the Vilest of Men, The Advocateship of Jesus Christ*, ed. Richard L. Greaves (Oxford: Oxford University Press, 1985), xxi.

53. Greaves, *Glimpses of Glory*, 597–99.

Toleration (1689) allowed for freedom of worship for Nonconformist Protestants. Ironically, as God's providence would have it, Bunyan died just before liberty arrived.

Bunyan's writings continued to issue from the presses in a steady stream. Of course, many books were published individually, especially *The Pilgrim's Progress*. Charles Doe edited a single-volume, folio edition of Bunyan's *Works* (1692), though this did not contain *The Pilgrim's Progress*, *Holy War*, and many other writings. In 1736 and 1737, a fuller edition of his *Works* appeared, edited by Ebenezer Chandler and Samuel Wilson. The yet more complete edition of Bunyan's *Works* was published in 1767 with a preface by George Whitefield. In 1853, George Offor edited a three-volume edition of the *Works*, which has been reprinted by the Banner of Truth Trust and is the most accessible edition today. In the latter part of the twentieth century, Roger Sharrock oversaw the printing of critical editions by Oxford University Press of *The Pilgrim's Progress*, *Grace Abounding*, *The Holy War*, *Mr. Badman*, and thirteen volumes of the *Miscellaneous Works* with scholarly introductions.

Just before Bunyan died, he delivered to the publisher the manuscript of *The Acceptable Sacrifice: Or the Excellency of a Broken Heart* (published 1689). It was based on Psalm 51:17: "The sacrifices of God are a broken spirit: a broken and a contrite heart, O God, thou wilt not despise." In many ways, this text captures Bunyan's spiritual pilgrimage. The preface by George Cokayn states that Bunyan's book "is but a transcript out of his own heart: for God (who had much work for him to do) was still hewing and hammering him by his Word, and sometimes also by more than ordinary temptations and desertions."[54] Bunyan said, "A broken heart is the handiwork of God. . . . By breaking of the heart, he opens it, and makes it

54. George Cokayn, "A Preface to the Reader," in John Bunyan, *The Acceptable Sacrifice: Or the Excellency of a Broken Heart* (London: George Larkin, 1689), A2v.

a receptacle for the graces of his Spirit; that's the cabinet, when unlocked, where God lays up the jewels of the gospel. There he puts his fear. . . . There he writes his law."[55]

We may thank God that He so broke the heart of John Bunyan as to make him a vessel fit to hold the priceless jewel of the fear of the Lord, for the church's enrichment. It is a wondrous thing to behold when God breaks a person so that the glory of Christ will shine brightly from his life for the good of others. Paul writes of it in 2 Corinthians 4:6–9, 12:

> God, who commanded the light to shine out of darkness, hath shined in our hearts, to give the light of the knowledge of the glory of God in the face of Jesus Christ. But we have this treasure in earthen vessels, that the excellency of the power may be of God, and not of us. We are troubled on every side, yet not distressed; we are perplexed, but not in despair; persecuted, but not forsaken; cast down, but not destroyed. . . . So then death worketh in us, but life in you.

Let us never fear to be broken by God. He breaks us to fill us with heavenly treasure and to fill the world with the fragrance of Christ.

55. Bunyan, *The Acceptable Sacrifice*, 150; see *Works*, 1:709.

3

The Dread and Terrible Majesty

A century after Bunyan sat in prison, the great evangelist George Whitefield (1714–1770) wrote a preface to a new edition of Bunyan's *Works*. Though a minister of the Church of England (the church that once persecuted Bunyan), Whitefield loved the writings of Bunyan and the Puritans. Whitefield exemplified the principles of the evangelical core of that church, and he devoted his life to preaching Christ to many thousands of people in Britain and America. He saw Bunyan as a beautiful example of free and sovereign grace—God's taking a lowly and wicked man and making him by the all-powerful work of the Holy Spirit to be a righteous and skillful scribe for the kingdom of God. Whitefield said that Bunyan's *Works* had been much used by God "in pulling down Satan's strongholds in sinners' hearts." Like the Bible commentaries of Matthew Henry and the writings of John Flavel and John Owen, the publication of Bunyan's *Works* was a joy to Whitefield, who longed for God alone to be glorified among mankind.[1]

1. George Whitefield, preface to *The Works of that Eminent Servant of Christ Mr. John Bunyan*, 3rd ed. (London: W. Johnston, 1767), 1:iii–iv.

What makes Bunyan's writings so helpful? Surely one reason is that Bunyan's writings are full of the words and truths of the Bible. And, like the Bible, Bunyan's books are permeated by a sense of the holiness of God. Whether writing a story about pilgrims or writing a treatise on biblical teachings, Bunyan took up his pen with a profound awareness that he lived in the presence of the righteous Lord of time and eternity.

The Infinite Majesty of God

Bunyan had a high view of God. He saw the fear of God as inseparable from God's nature. "Who would not fear thee, O King of nations?" (Jer. 10:7). Even God's grace inspires fear (see Ps. 130:4), for God is always God. Thus, for Bunyan, godliness is always theological—rooted in the knowledge of God. He feared God because he knew God.

Who is this God? Bunyan wrote, "God is a Spirit, eternal, infinite, incomprehensible, perfect, and unspeakably glorious in his being, attributes and works: the eternal God." Even when men speak truly of God's "attributes," such as "wisdom, power, justice, holiness, mercy, etc.," God is far beyond human understanding, "inconceivably perfect and infinite." We may speak of different attributes, but in reality they are not parts of God, but one in the simplicity of the divine being. Even the angels have no direct vision of God's essential glory, for the Lord is "known in the perfection of his being only to himself."[2]

It may surprise the reader that a tinker would use such theological language in speaking of the Lord. Bunyan had drunk at the stream of Reformed orthodoxy, that heritage of doctrine flowing from the Scriptures through the writings of the Reformers and

2. John Bunyan, *Exposition on the Ten First Chapters of Genesis, and Part of the Eleventh*, in *Works* (1692), 1; see *Works*, 2:414. The margin cites John 4:24; Job 11:7; Deut. 33:27; Heb. 4:12–13; Prov. 15:11; Rom. 1:20; Gen. 17:1; Isa. 6:2; Ex. 33:20 [some references corrected]. For a similar statement, see John Bunyan, *A Confession of My Faith, and A Reason of My Practice* (London: Francis Smith, 1672), 1–2, in *Works*, 2:594.

Puritans. Compare his statement to the famous description of God in the Westminster Shorter Catechism (1647): "God is a Spirit, infinite, eternal, and unchangeable, in his being, wisdom, power, holiness, justice, goodness, and truth."[3] Likewise, the Belgic Confession (1561) declares that God is "eternal, incomprehensible, invisible, immutable, infinite, almighty, perfectly wise, just, good, and the overflowing fountain of all good."[4]

Most significantly, Bunyan got his view of the majesty of the Lord directly from the Holy Scriptures. Bunyan gloried in the God of the Bible. Drawing on Hebrews 1:2–3, Isaiah 40:15, Jeremiah 23:24, and Proverbs 15:3, he proclaimed,

> the true and living God, Maker of the worlds, and upholder of all things by the word of his power; that incomprehensible Majesty, in comparison of whom, all nations are less than the drop of a bucket, and . . . the small dust of the balance. This is he that fills heaven and earth, and is everywhere present with the children of men, beholding the evil and the good; for he has set his eyes upon all their ways.[5]

The proper human response to such a glorious God is to fear Him, as the Old and New Testaments repeatedly command us (see Eccl. 12:13; 1 Peter 1:17; Rev. 14:7).[6] Gracious fear causes the heart to "stand in awe both of the mercies and judgments of God" and keeps it in an attitude of "reverence of the heavenly majesty."[7] Greaves writes,

3. Westminster Shorter Catechism (Q. 4), in *Reformed Confessions of the Sixteenth and Seventeenth Centuries in English Translation*, vol. 4, *1600–1693*, ed. James T. Dennison Jr. (Grand Rapids: Reformation Heritage Books, 2014), 353. The identical statement was adopted by the Particular Baptists in their 1693 catechism (p. 574).

4. Belgic Confession (Art. 1), in *Reformed Confessions of the Sixteenth and Seventeenth Centuries in English Translation*, vol. 2, *1552–1566*, ed. James T. Dennison Jr. (Grand Rapids: Reformation Heritage Books, 2010), 425.

5. John Bunyan, *A Treatise of the Fear of God* (London: N. Ponder, 1679), 1–2; see *Works*, 1:437–38.

6. Bunyan, *A Treatise of the Fear of God*, 1; see *Works*, 1:437.

7. Bunyan, *A Treatise of the Fear of God*, 90; see *Works*, 1:458.

"For Bunyan the divine nature was holiness"; this perception "was in large measure responsible for generating in man a fear of God."[8]

Bunyan's emphasis on the fear of the Lord was not unusual for preachers and writers of that era.[9] He could easily have learned it from Lewis Bayly (c. 1575–1631), author of *The Practice of Piety*, which was half of Bunyan's original two-book library of godly writers. This book may well have shaped Bunyan's doctrine of God.[10] Bayly placed special emphasis on awe, fear, and reverence as the proper "use" or practical application of the knowledge of God. God reveals Himself in His Word

> to possess our hearts with a greater awe of his majesty, whilst we admire him for his simpleness and infiniteness: adore him for his unmeasurableness, unchangeableness, and eternity: seek wisdom from his understanding and knowledge: submit ourselves to his blessed will and pleasure: love him, and his love, mercy, goodness, and patience: trust to his Word, because of his truth: fear him for his power, justice, and anger; reverence him for his holiness: and praise him for his blessedness: and to depend all our life on him, who is the only author of our life, being, and all the good things we have.[11]

The knowledge of God is given to us "that we may in our prayers and meditations conceive aright of his divine majesty." If people knew who God is, Bayly said, they would not "make an idol out of the true God" and participate in religious activities "with so much irreverence

8. Richard L. Greaves, *John Bunyan*, Courtenay Studies in Reformation Theology 2 (Grand Rapids: Eerdmans, 1969), 29–30.

9. Geoffrey F. Nuttall, review of *The Miscellaneous Works of John Bunyan, Volume IX, A Treatise of the Fear of God; The Greatness of the Soul; A Holy Life*, ed. Richard L. Greaves, *Religious Studies* 18, no. 4 (December 1982): 550.

10. Richard L. Greaves, introduction to *The Miscellaneous Works of John Bunyan*, vol. 2, *The Doctrine of the Law and Grace Unfolded and I Will Pray with the Spirit*, ed. Richard L. Greaves (Oxford: Oxford University Press, 1976), xvii–xviii.

11. Lewis Bayly, *The Practice of Pietie* (London: Robert Allot, 1633), 45; see Lewis Bayly, *The Practice of Piety* (1842; repr., Morgan, PA: Soli Deo Gloria, 1994), 24.

and hypocrisy," but instead would worship and "serve him with fear and reverence: for so far does a man fear God, as he knows him."[12]

Likewise, Martin Luther's commentary on Galatians, so helpful to Bunyan in his spiritual struggles, said, "We must trust and glory in God alone. He only is to be loved, he only is to be feared and honored."[13] The Genevan Reformer John Calvin (1509–1564) said that "piety" or godliness is "that reverence joined with love of God which the knowledge of his benefits induces"; the first thing our knowledge of God should teach us is "fear and reverence."[14] Like the Reformers and Puritans, Bunyan saw fear as an essential element of true godliness. Without "reverence and godly fear," we cannot "serve God acceptably" (Heb. 12:28).[15]

Fear is so closely joined with the knowledge of God, Bunyan wrote, that one of God's titles is the "Fear" of His people—namely, "the Fear of Isaac" (Gen. 31:42, 53)—because of "the dread and terrible majesty that is in him" (see Deut. 7:21; 10:17; Neh. 1:5; 4:14; 9:32; Job 37:22).[16] Bunyan used the word "dread" not in a negative sense, meaning abhorrent or appallingly evil, but in the sense of causing great fear and awe. God is inescapably awe inspiring.

This emphasis raises a question about Bunyan's view of God. Was he guilty of legalism? Did his view of God put people into bondage instead of bringing them into the liberty of the gospel? In the next chapter, we will see that Bunyan did not believe that Christians should live in bondage to fear. At this point, it is enough to say that Bunyan believed and taught that the fearfully majestic Lord is also the loving Savior. In fact, Bunyan titled one of his books *Come, and Welcome, to Jesus Christ.*

12. Bayly, *The Practice of Pietie* (1633), 46–47; see *The Practice of Piety* (1994), 25.

13. Luther, *Galatians*, fol. 50v.

14. John Calvin, *Institutes of the Christian Religion*, ed. John T. McNeill, trans. Ford Lewis Battles, The Library of Christian Classics 20, 21 (Philadelphia: Westminster Press, 1960), 1.2.1–2.

15. Bunyan, *A Treatise of the Fear of God*, 2; see *Works*, 1:438.

16. Bunyan, *A Treatise of the Fear of God*, 4; see *Works*, 1:438.

How can a holy and just God release sinners from damnation and the terrors of hell? God does so by giving them a righteousness that perfectly satisfies His justice. Bunyan taught that God, having rejected man's imperfect righteousness, has substituted in its place "the glorious righteousness of his Son," which is "perfect and equal to his justice and holiness." Jesus Christ is equal to God, separated from all sin, and free from all guilt (see Phil. 2:6; Heb. 7:26; 1 Peter 2:22).[17] The righteousness of Christ's obedience has two aspects: first, "in a doing of that which the law commands us to do"; secondly, "in a paying that price for the transgression thereof, which justice has said shall be required at the hand of man; and that is the cursed death."[18] Bunyan here used the theological distinction between the active and the passive obedience of Christ: the Lord Jesus kept the law's precepts for His people and suffered the law's punishment for His people.

God then applies Christ's merit to sinners by faith. "By an act of the sovereign grace of God," God counts Christ's perfect righteousness to "the sinner that shall dare to trust thereto [in it] for justification from the curse of the law" (see 1 Cor. 1:30; 2 Cor. 5:21).[19] Faith is not the Christian's righteousness, but is the instrument of his justification. Bunyan said that Christians must carefully distinguish between "the meritorious, and the instrumental cause of their justification. Christ with what he has done and suffered is the meritorious cause of our justification," for His obedience alone is the believer's righteousness that satisfies God's justice (see Rom. 5:9–10). Our faith does not deserve God's blessing but "is given by God to those whom he saves, that thereby they may embrace and put on that Christ, by whose righteousness they must be saved."[20]

17. John Bunyan, *A Discourse upon the Pharisee and the Publicane* (London: Joh. Harris, 1685), 41; see *Works*, 2:229.

18. Bunyan, *A Discourse upon the Pharisee and the Publicane*, 99; see *Works*, 2:247.

19. Bunyan, *A Discourse upon the Pharisee and the Publicane*, 42; see *Works*, 2:229.

20. John Bunyan, *Saved by Grace: Or, A Discourse of the Grace of God*, in *Works* (1692), 556; see *Works*, 1:339

Bunyan's use of the language of *causes* is rooted in a form of logic derived from the philosophy of Aristotle and widely used in theological discussions of his day.[21] His use of this terminology agrees with what other Reformed writers said. Calvin identified Christ and his obedience as the *material cause* and faith as the *instrumental cause* of justification and salvation, comparing faith to an empty vessel or open mouth by which sinners receive the grace of Christ.[22] John Owen wrote that most Protestant theologians "affirmed faith to be the instrumental cause of our justification." Owen also said that "Christ alone" is "the meritorious cause" of justification.[23] What this means is that faith does not earn anything from God by its own worthiness, but simply receives the gift of what Christ accomplished.

Bunyan positioned himself in the center of the doctrine of justification by faith alone as taught by the churches of the Reformation. Though not a member of the Church of England, he affirmed as one of the "fundamental truths of the Christian religion" the statement in its Thirty-Nine Articles (1563): "We are accounted righteous before God, only for the merit of our Lord and Savior Jesus Christ, by faith, and not for our own works, or deserving; wherefore that we are justified by faith only, is a most wholesome doctrine, and full of comfort."[24] Ironically, Bunyan took this position in opposition to Latitudinarians *within* the Church of England, who held that Christ was a moral example, taught that God justified sinners because of their sincere resolution to obey Him, and identified righteousness as the rule of human reason over the body and emotions to keep the laws of God.[25]

21. See Richard A. Muller, *Dictionary of Latin and Greek Theological Terms: Drawn Principally from Protestant Scholastic Theology* (Grand Rapids: Baker, 1985), 61.

22. Calvin, *Institutes*, 3.11.7; 3.14.17, 21.

23. John Owen, *The Doctrine of Justification by Faith*, in *The Works of John Owen*, ed. William H. Goold (1850–1853; repr., Edinburgh, UK: Banner of Truth, 1965), 5:108, 284.

24. John Bunyan, *A Defence of the Doctrine of Justification, By Faith in Jesus Christ Shewing, True Gospel-Holiness Flows from Thence* (London: Francis Smith, 1673), 113; see *Works*, 2:332. See the Thirty-Nine Articles (art. 11), in Dennison, *Reformed Confessions*, 2:758.

25. Isabel Rivers, "Grace, Holiness, and the Pursuit of Happiness: Bunyan and Restoration Latitudinarianism," in *John Bunyan: Conventicle and Parnassus; Tercentenary Essays*,

Bunyan taught that the true Christian will do good works, but insisted that works have no place in our justification and righteousness before God. He said, "Not that faith needs good works as an help to justification before God. For in this matter faith will be ignorant of all good works, except those done by the person of Christ."[26] In this, he echoed Luther's commentary on Galatians, which said, "The greatest knowledge then, and the greatest wisdom of Christians is . . . to be ignorant of works . . . especially when the conscience wrestles with the judgment of God."[27] This repudiation of one's own good works is not easy, Bunyan said, because it is devastating to our pride. A person must submit to the cross to receive it: "A man is forced to suffer the destruction of his own righteousness for the righteousness of another."[28]

Though faith in Christ alone is difficult, and the doctrine of justification profound, the basic message of the gospel is simple and clear. Bunyan showed his grasp of the simplicity of the gospel message in the second part of *The Pilgrim's Progress*, the story of Christian's wife and family following him to the Celestial City. At one point, Prudence questions the children of Christiana regarding their understanding of the faith. We can weave her questions and the boys' answers together into a simple gospel catechism:

Q. Can you tell who made you?
A. God the Father, God the Son, and God the Holy Ghost.

Q. What is man?
A. A reasonable creature, so made by God.

---

ed. N. H. Keeble (Oxford: Clarendon Press, 1988), 57–59.

26. John Bunyan, introduction to *A Holy Life, The Beauty of Christianity* (London: by B. W. for Benj. Alsop, 1684), sig. A3r; see *Works*, 2:507.

27. Luther, "The Argument," in *Galatians*, fol. 6r.

28. John Bunyan, *The Heavenly Foot-man: Or, A Description of the Man that Gets to Heaven* (London: Charles Doe, 1698), 30; see *Works*, 3:386.

Q. What is supposed by this word, *saved*?
A. That man by sin has brought himself into a state of captivity and misery.

Q. And can you tell who saves you?
A. God the Father, God the Son, and God the Holy Ghost.

Q. What is supposed by [man's] being saved by the Trinity?
A. That sin is so great and mighty a tyrant, that none can pull us out of its clutches but God, and that God is good and loving to man, as to pull him indeed out of his miserable state.

Q. But how does God the Father save you?
A. By his grace.

Q. How does God the Son save you?
A. By his righteousness, death, and blood, and life.

Q. And how does God the Holy Ghost save you?
A. By his illumination, by his renovation, and by his preservation.

Q. What is God's design in saving of poor men?
A. The glorifying of his name, of his grace, and justice, etc. And the everlasting happiness of his creature.

Q. Who are they that must be saved?
A. Those that accept of his salvation.[29]

Before we continue our exploration of Bunyan's teaching, you should pause here and ask yourself a question. Do you know this

29. See John Bunyan, *The Pilgrim's Progress, From This World to That Which Is to Come: The Second Part* (London: Nathaniel Ponder, 1684), 76–78; also *Works*, 3:199.

God? We all have an idea or image of God in our minds, but it is often sadly distorted. Some people view God as a heavenly grandfather who accepts everyone unconditionally and winks at our sins. Others view God as a malicious policeman who is watching for an opportunity to catch you doing something wrong. In reality, as Bunyan reminds us, the God of the Bible is a God of fearsome majesty and amazing grace.

Do you know God personally? That is to say, do you know Him in a way that engages your heart to trust in Jesus Christ alone as your righteousness? If you do, then God has planted love for Him and fear toward Him in your heart. God is no longer a distant Supreme Being. You now live in the presence of the living God.

In His Glorious Presence

God's presence moves people with holy dread, even when He comes with the comforting and joyous news of mercy and salvation. To illustrate this, Bunyan reminded his readers of Jacob's dream of a ladder that reached from heaven to earth. God spoke to Jacob, not in wrath and fury, but "in the most sweet and gracious manner," giving him several promises of good. How did Jacob respond? He said, "Surely the LORD is in this place; and I knew it not. And he was afraid, and said, How dreadful is this place! this is none other but the house of God, and this is the gate of heaven" (Gen. 28:16–17). Bunyan noted, "All the grace that discovered [revealed] itself in this heavenly vision to him could not keep him from dread and fear of God's majesty."[30] If the angels evoke fear when they come with messages of grace to mankind, how much more awe-inspiring is God? Bunyan exclaimed, "Man crumbles to dust at the presence of God, yea though he shows himself to us in his robes of salvation."[31]

30. Bunyan, *A Treatise of the Fear of God*, 5; see *Works*, 1:438.
31. Bunyan, *A Treatise of the Fear of God*, 6; see *Works*, 1:439.

Though this combination of grace and fear may seem strange to many modern Christians, who think of the fear of God only in connection to punishment, Puritan theology commonly linked fear to God's glory, not just to His punishment. William Ames (1576–1633) wrote that the fear of God is praiseworthy "when we revere the majesty and power of God, so that the principal cause of our fear is not any evil which we are in danger of, but the excellent perfection of God."[32] Ames cited the Jacob's ladder and "Fear of Isaac" texts (Gen. 28:17; 31:42, 53) as proofs of this statement—both of which Bunyan used in close proximity for the same purpose. Ames's book on the conscience was popular among Nonconformists; Richard Baxter (1615–1691) included it in his top ten recommendations for a pastor's library.[33]

Why is God's presence so dreadful? Bunyan gave three reasons. First, God reveals His own "greatness and majesty," which is beyond human comprehension or endurance. When Christ appeared in a vision to John, the apostle "fell at his feet as dead" (Rev. 1:17).[34] Even when God makes known "the love of Christ, which passeth knowledge," such knowledge includes a sense of the infinite "breadth, and length, and depth, and height" of God's glory (Eph. 3:18–19). Therefore, Bunyan argued, the knowledge of God in Christ produces "an holy fear and reverence of this great God in our souls." Citing Revelation 15:4, he said, "Greatness should beget fear, greatness should beget reverence: now who so great as our God, and so, who to be feared like Him!"[35]

To know the Lord is to fear Him. God's name—that is, the revelation of His nature—is inherently awe inspiring. God's name is

32. William Ames, *Conscience with the Power and Cases Thereof*, 3.3, in *The Workes of the Reverend and Faithfull Minister of Christ William Ames* (London: John Rothwell, 1643), 51 [pagination irregular].

33. Richard Baxter, *A Christian Directory* (1864; repr., Morgan, PA: Soli Deo Gloria, 1996), 732.

34. Bunyan, *A Treatise of the Fear of God*, 7; see *Works*, 1:439.

35. John Bunyan, *The Saints Knowledge of Christ's Love, Or, The Unsearchable Riches of Christ*, in *Works* (1692), 412; see *Works*, 2:13.

"glorious and fearful" (Deut. 28:58), "holy and reverend" (Ps. 111:9). The righteous desire and pray "to fear thy name" with all their hearts (Ps. 86:11), and God has resolved that all nations shall fear the name of the Lord because He is the great King (see Ps. 102:15; Mal. 1:6, 11, 14). God is pleased when men fear Him, and He will show His pleasure when He rewards those who fear His name at the coming of Christ to judge the world (see Rev. 11:18).[36]

Second, God's presence is fearful because, when we see God's glory, we see ourselves as we truly are. Like Daniel, all our beauty is turned to "corruption" (Dan. 10:8). Our best works are revealed to be "polluted rags," and the glory of our "candle" disappears in "the clear light of the shining sun." This was the experience of Isaiah, who had a vision of God's holiness and exclaimed, "Woe is me! For I am undone; because I am a man of unclean lips, and I dwell in the midst of a people of unclean lips: for mine eyes have seen the King, the LORD of hosts" (Isa. 6:5). Even though this was a "vision of his Savior," it gave him a greater sense of the immense difference between God and him, especially in his sinful nature.[37]

Bunyan's doctrine on this point resembles the teaching of Calvin in the opening sections of his *Institutes of the Christian Religion*, mediated to Bunyan through the Puritans. Calvin wrote that we humans are self-confident and self-righteous until we begin to have some true thoughts of God. Then, as a man who looks at the sun is overwhelmed with its brightness, so the knowledge of God's perfect righteousness, wisdom, and power dazzles us; and in that light we can see our wickedness, foolishness, and weakness.[38] Calvin wrote, "Hence that dread and wonder with which Scripture commonly represents the saints as stricken and overcome whenever they felt the presence of God."[39]

36. Bunyan, *A Treatise of the Fear of God*, 12–14; see *Works*, 1:440.
37. Bunyan, *A Treatise of the Fear of God*, 8–9; see *Works*, 1:439.
38. Calvin, *Institutes*, 1.1.2.
39. Calvin, *Institutes*, 1.1.3.

Men respond with humble fear not to a merely intellectual idea of God, but only when they have a spiritual *sense* of God's glory. Bunyan used sensory language for spiritual experience. He taught in *The Acceptable Sacrifice* that the repentant man has "all the senses of his soul" alive and active, whereas "others are dead and senseless."[40] He "sees" the sinfulness of his nature, "feels" in his heart the pain of God's hatred of transgression, "hears" the bad news of his corrupt condition, "smells" the offensive stink of his sins, and "tastes" the bitterness of his evil lusts.[41] This spiritual sense of his own depravity springs from a spiritual sense of God's glory. Bunyan said, "A man cannot be sorry for the sinful defects of nature, till he sees they have rendered him contemptible to God; nor is it anything but a sight of God, that can make him truly see what he is, and so be heartily sorry for being so. . . . Visions of God break the heart."[42] He wrote, "This therefore, is the cause of a broken heart; even a sight of divine excellencies."[43] It is not the sight that belongs to the wicked and damned, however, but a spiritual sense accompanied by love for God and hatred for evil.[44] The believer is deeply grieved for his sins and humbled in God's presence precisely because he loves God.

A spiritual sight of God's beauty calls forth both love and fear. In *A Holy Life, The Beauty of Christianity*, Bunyan said that saving faith "apprehends the truth of the being and greatness of God, and so it awes the spirit of a man" and "apprehends the sweetness and blessedness of the nature of the Godhead," and therefore persuades the person to desire communion with God in holiness in this life and enjoyment of God in the world to come.[45] When the town of Mansoul sent Mr. Desires-awake to ask for mercy from

40. John Bunyan, *The Acceptable Sacrifice: Or the Excellency of a Broken Heart* (London: George Larkin, 1689), 50; see *Works* 1:696.

41. Bunyan, *The Acceptable Sacrifice*, 50–59; see *Works* 1:696–97.

42. Bunyan, *The Acceptable Sacrifice*, 62; see *Works* 1:697.

43. Bunyan, *The Acceptable Sacrifice*, 65; see *Works* 1:698.

44. Bunyan, *The Acceptable Sacrifice*, 66; see *Works* 1:698.

45. Bunyan, *A Holy Life*, 41; see *Works*, 2:519.

Prince Emmanuel, their messenger returned and said, "The Prince to whom you sent me, is such a one for beauty and glory, that whoever sees him must both love and fear him."[46]

Many Puritans used sensory language for spiritual experience, and later Jonathan Edwards (1703–1758) would develop in great depth the doctrine of "a sense of the heart of the supreme beauty" of God's holiness.[47] Edwards also said that this "discovery of God's holy beauty" produces "evangelical humiliation" by which believers count themselves "contemptible" for their sinfulness and "are brought sweetly to yield, and freely and with delight to prostrate themselves at the feet of God."[48] Edwards' book catalog shows that he was aware of Bunyan's *Acceptable Sacrifice* and had an interest in it,[49] but we should not infer any direct influence. Rather, Bunyan and Edwards were both influenced by the Reformers and Puritans. Once again, we see that Bunyan kept at least one foot planted in the stream of Reformed orthodoxy.

Third, God's presence is fearful because God reveals His goodness. This may seem like a contradiction to the modern mind, where God's goodness and love are generally assumed to promote a casual attitude toward Him. Bunyan knew of people in his own day whom he called "light, frothy" Christians. They acted as if the presence of God and the sense of His grace in Christ moves men to do "antics" more like "a fool of a play" than like those in the presence of the God who is infinitely greater than any earthly king.[50] However, Bunyan again shows how different the mind-set of the Spirit is from the

46. John Bunyan, *The Holy War, Made by Shaddai upon Diabolus . . . Or, the Losing and Taking Again of the Town of Mansoul* (London: Nat. Ponder, 1696), 130; see *Works*, 3:299. The original reads "whoso" instead of "whoever."

47. Jonathan Edwards, *Religious Affections*, in *The Works of Jonathan Edwards*, vol. 2, *Religious Affections*, ed. John E. Smith (New Haven, CT: Yale University Press, 1959), 272. For the language of spiritual sensation in the Puritans, see Brad Walton, *Jonathan Edwards,* Religious Affections *and the Puritan Analysis of True Piety, Spiritual Sensation and Heart Religion*, Studies in American Religion 74 (Lewiston, NY: Edwin Mellen Press, 2002), 197–206.

48. Edwards, *Religious Affections*, in *The Works of Jonathan Edwards*, 2:312.

49. Jonathan Edwards, "'Catalogue' of Reading," in *The Works of Jonathan Edwards*, vol. 26, *Catalogues of Books*, ed. Peter J. Thuesen (New Haven, CT: Yale University Press, 2008), 128.

50. Bunyan, *A Treatise of the Fear of God*, 11; see *Works*, 1:440.

mind-set of the flesh. He quotes Hosea 3:5, a promise that God's repentant people will "fear the LORD and his goodness." Bunyan comments, "The goodness as well as the greatness of God does beget in the heart of his elect an awful reverence of his majesty."[51] God's sovereign power in protecting us should fill us with fear (see Jer. 5:22). God's forgiveness and goodness move people to fear and tremble (see Jer. 33:8–9). Why would grace inspire fear? Bunyan explained that even when God comes in forgiveness and love, "God must appear like himself," and so "the beams of his majesty" shine in His saving works. Salvation does not hide God's awesome glory but reveals it even more grandly than before.[52]

There is something amazing in grace, for the infinitely glorious God has gone to such infinite lengths to save sinners. Bunyan exclaimed, "Oh! That a great God should be a good God; a good God to an unworthy, to an undeserving, and to a people that continually do what they can to provoke the eyes of His glory; this should make us tremble."[53]

Someone might object, "Shouldn't we rejoice when God forgives our sins?" Bunyan answered with Scripture: "Rejoice with trembling" (Ps. 2:11). "Solid and godly joy" fits very well with tearful eyes that weep over sins. Bunyan explained that when God comes and gives a sinner forgiveness of his sins, this grace "removes the guilt, but increases the sense of your filth, and the sense of this that God has forgiven a filthy sinner will make you both rejoice and tremble."[54] He quoted Ezekiel 16:63, a promise to those brought into everlasting covenant with the Lord (see v. 60) that they will be humbled and silenced because of their shame *when God has been pacified for their sins.*

In this point, Bunyan has deployed a theological distinction commonly made between the "stain" (*macula*) of sin upon the soul

51. Bunyan, *A Treatise of the Fear of God*, 10; see *Works*, 1:439.
52. Bunyan, *A Treatise of the Fear of God*, 10–11; see *Works*, 1:439–40.
53. Bunyan, *The Saints Knowledge*, in *Works* (1692), 412; see *Works*, 2:14.
54. Bunyan, *A Treatise of the Fear of God*, 12; see *Works*, 1:440.

as long as sin remains, and the "guilt" (*reatus*) or liability to punishment that God removes when He forgives sin. This distinction appears in writings of the medieval theologian Thomas Aquinas (1225–1274) and Reformed orthodox theologians such as Isaac Ambrose (1604–1664) and John Owen, the last of whom was a friend of Bunyan.[55] Without having been trained in the technical Latin terms, Bunyan nevertheless had adopted the theological concept and used it to pastorally guide souls into a right combination of joy and fear in the presence of God. The believer can rejoice that God has forgiven him through Christ and will never punish him as his sins deserve. However, the believer still has cause for great humility and shame in God's presence because he is not yet completely like Christ, and because sin still stains his soul with moral filth.

This in no way diminishes the goodness of God's presence, but accentuates it. It is precisely because God's presence is so good that it humbles us. However, God's presence is still the desire and delight of believers. Bunyan exclaimed, "What, what shall I say? God's presence is renewing, transforming, seasoning, sanctifying, commanding, sweetening, and enlightening to the soul. Nothing is like it in all the world."[56]

Acceptable Worship with Reverence and Godly Fear

Whenever you think or speak of God, you should do so "with reverence and godly fear" (Heb. 12:28) or, as Bunyan said, "with great dread of his majesty upon your hearts, and in great soberness and

55. Thomas Aquinas, *Summa Theologica, Part 2 (First Part)*, trans. Fathers of the English Dominican Province (London: R. & T. Washbourne, 1915), Q. 85–87; Isaac Ambrose, *Looking unto Jesus* (Pittsburgh: Luke Loomis, 1823), 123; John Owen, *The Doctrine of Justification by Faith*, in *Works*, 5:199. Medieval theologians made a further distinction between guilt of blameworthiness (*reatus culpae*) and guilt of punishment (*reatus poenae*), which Ambrose accepted but Owen rejected. See Charles Hodge, *Systematic Theology* (repr., Peabody, MA: Hendrickson, 1999), 2:188–89; Herman Bavinck, *Reformed Dogmatics*, ed. John Bolt, trans. John Vriend (Grand Rapids: Baker Academic, 2006), 3:171.

56. John Bunyan, *The Desire of the Righteous Granted*, in *Works* (1692), 241; see *Works*, 1:756. The original reads "lightning" instead of "enlightening."

truth." It is especially offensive to preach, pray, swear oaths in God's name, or converse with other people about the things of God in a frivolous and lighthearted manner as if the Lord were trivial. God is jealous over the glory that we owe to His name (see Ex. 20:7; Lev. 20:3).[57]

Sinners and legalists commonly engage in prayer and worship "with senselessness of the majesty of God." They are unaware that God is a consuming fire and that unforgiven sinners are "as stubble fully dry." Bunyan wrote, "Their blindness gives them boldness."[58] A person should pray deeply conscious of "the infinite distance between God and him," and worshipers should "tremble in the thoughts of it when they are about to approach the Omnipotent Presence."[59] Therefore, we must beware of rushing into God's presence, rashly speaking to God, and forgetting the infinite difference between us and Him, but should instead humbly rely upon the mediation of our Great High Priest, Jesus Christ.[60]

If God's nature and presence are intrinsically fearsome, then human beings should offer up the service of His worship with holy reverence. Bunyan in this regard quoted Psalm 5:7, "But as for me, I will come into thy house in the multitude of thy mercy: and in thy fear will I worship toward thy holy temple," and Psalm 2:11, "Serve the LORD with fear, and rejoice with trembling."[61] Bunyan evidently believed that knowing God's love and mercy, and rejoicing in His goodness, are perfectly consistent with fearing and trembling before Him.

God's worship is a fearful activity because, Bunyan said, "it is the worship of *God*." The Lord is in a category infinitely above us.

57. Bunyan, *A Treatise of the Fear of God*, 15; see *Works*, 1:441.

58. John Bunyan, *A Discourse upon the Pharisee and the Publicane*, 174–75; see *Works*, 2:269.

59. Bunyan, *A Discourse upon the Pharisee and the Publicane*, 177; see *Works*, 2:269. The word "between" in the first quote is "betwixt" in the original.

60. Bunyan, *A Discourse upon the Pharisee and the Publicane*, 178; see *Works*, 2:270.

61. Bunyan, *A Treatise of the Fear of God*, 16; see *Works*, 1:441.

Bunyan lived in a world of hierarchy, where children served parents, servants served masters, and subjects served noblemen and kings. We should serve each person with the measure of respect fitting to his rank (see Rom. 13:7). How much reverence then should fill our service of the God who is "so great and dreadful in himself"?[62]

Furthermore, Bunyan said, "this glorious Majesty is himself present to behold his worshipers in their worshiping him." The Lord Jesus promised that when the church gathers, "There am I in the midst" (Matt. 18:20; see also Ps. 22:22). This promise is a comforting thought for believers, but Bunyan draws upon the vision of Revelation to remind his readers that Christ's presence is also a matter of awe: "He is said to walk in the midst of the seven golden candlesticks (Rev. 1), that is, in the church, and that with a countenance like the sun, with a head and hair as white as snow; and with eyes like a flame of fire. This puts dread and fear into his service."[63] Too often the church worships God with little apparent awareness of whose presence they are in.

God's love for His glory moves Him to burn with holy zeal for His worship. Bunyan wrote, "God is jealous of his worship." He notes that in only one of the Ten Commandments does God declare Himself to be a jealous God: the commandment on how we worship (see Ex. 20:4–6).[64] God's jealousy is not an idle thing. God killed two of His priests, Nadab and Abihu (see Lev. 10:1–3), because they did not honor God as holy by doing "nothing in his worship but what is well-pleasing to him." Similarly God struck dead Eli's sons, Uzza, and Ananias and Sapphira for failing to serve God with fear (see 1 Sam. 2; 1 Chron. 13; Acts 5).[65]

Bunyan said that the fearfulness of worship rebukes three kinds of people. First, it rebukes those who do not worship God at all. They

62. Bunyan, *A Treatise of the Fear of God*, 17; see *Works*, 1:441.
63. Bunyan, *A Treatise of the Fear of God*, 18; see *Works*, 1:441.
64. Bunyan, *A Treatise of the Fear of God*, 18; see *Works*, 1:441.
65. Bunyan, *A Treatise of the Fear of God*, 19; see *Works*, 1:442.

have no reverence for God's majesty, nor do they honor the Most High God in the congregation of His people. Therefore, God will pour out His wrath and fury upon them (see Ps. 79:6; Jer. 10:25). Second, it rebukes those who think it is enough to be physically present in public worship but who pay no attention to the attitude of their hearts. Some come to church to sleep, to make business connections, to enjoy "the wicked fellowship of their vain companion," or to look lustfully upon those whom they find sexually attractive. God will damn them because they do not come to worship God with reverential fear. Third, it rebukes those who do not care how they worship, but whose worship is based merely on the "precept of men," and so is "a stink in the nostrils of God" (see Isa. 29:13–14; Matt. 15:7–9).[66]

What then of the boldness and freedom of the children of God? Is the worship of the saints a miserable cowering before God's majesty? Not at all. To the contrary, Bunyan taught that the fear of the Lord gives a person "boldness . . . in his approaches into the presence of God." He proves this surprising conclusion by quoting Nehemiah 1:11: "O Lord, I beseech thee, let now thine ear be attentive to the prayer of thy servant, and to the prayer of thy servants, who desire to fear thy name." Why would the fear of God encourage bold prayers, as it did for Nehemiah? Bunyan's answer is that "God had promised before to 'bless them that fear him, both small and great'" (see Ps. 115:13).[67] Godly fear joins forces with faith in God's promises to strengthen prayer with confidence. Reverence and confidence are not enemies, but friends.

Bunyan's stories are full of reverence but also full of singing and joy. Those received into the church find that there is "music in the house, music in the heart, and music also in heaven, for joy that we are here."[68] The Bible is bad news only for the Devil and for those who insist on following him. The gospel of Christ is like

66. Bunyan, *A Treatise of the Fear of God*, 20–21; see *Works*, 1:442.
67. Bunyan, *A Treatise of the Fear of God*, 192–93; see *Works*, 1:481.
68. Bunyan, *The Pilgrim's Progress . . . The Second Part*, 73; see *Works*, 3:198.

the strings of an instrument "which, if but touched will such music make, they'll make a cripple dance, a giant quake."[69]

The key to drawing near to a holy God with boldness is Jesus Christ. Those who have been justified by Christ's righteousness and sanctified by the Holy Spirit's new birth can approach God boldly by exercising faith in Christ and His shed blood (see Heb. 4:16; 10:19–22). Bunyan said, "There is no boldness, godly boldness, but by blood. . . . It is the blood, the power of it by faith upon the conscience, that drives away guilt, and so fear; and consequently that begets boldness."[70] Though God's attributes of justice and holiness are by nature "set against sin and sinners," and though God is infinitely above us in glory in all His attributes, "yet by the passion of Jesus Christ, they harmoniously agree in the salvation of our souls." God engages all of His attributes to love those in Christ: "His justice is turned with wisdom, power, holiness, and truth, to love, yea, to love those that be found in his Son; forasmuch as there is nothing fault-worthy in His righteousness which is put upon us."[71]

Yet just as the river of the water of life flows from God's throne (see Rev. 22:1), so God's grace in Christ is full of God's reigning majesty. Bunyan said, "And indeed there is nothing in heaven or earth that can so awe the heart, as the grace of God. 'Tis that which makes a man fear, 'tis that which makes a man tremble, 'tis that which makes a man bow and bend, and break to pieces. Nothing has that majesty, and commanding greatness in and upon the hearts of the sons of men, as has the grace of God."[72] Therefore, by faith in the blood of Christ, the worshiper may be fearless of condemnation and simultaneously be full of holy fear.

69. Bunyan, "The Author's Way of Sending Forth His Second Part of the Pilgrim," in *The Pilgrim's Progress . . . The Second Part*, A6r; see *Works*, 3:170.

70. John Bunyan, *The Saints' Privilege and Profit*, in *Works* (1692), 270; see *Works*, 1:660.

71. Bunyan, *The Saints Knowledge of Christ's Love*, in *Works* (1692), 403; see *Works*, 2:3–4.

72. John Bunyan, *The Water of Life* (London: Nathanael Ponder, 1688), 39; see *Works*, 3:546–47.

4

Sinful and Preparatory Fears toward God

In Bunyan's tale *The Holy War*, after Diabolus has persuaded the town of Mansoul to turn against its good king and let him control it, the demonic tyrant fills it with evil. Diabolus rules Mansoul in sinful peace—except from time to time when Mr. Conscience disturbs it. However, when Diabolus hears that its former king, Shaddai, intends to recapture it, Diabolus equips its inhabitants for war. He gives a deceptive speech to Mansoul, claiming that Shaddai's army will show no mercy to those who surrender and desires only to murder and destroy: "Blood, blood, nothing but blood is in every blast of Shaddai's trumpet against poor Mansoul now."[1] The demon also gives his servants a "breastplate of iron," that is, a hard heart, and a "shield" of unbelief so that Shaddai's promises of mercy to those who repent will not win them and his warnings of judgment on rebels will not frighten them.[2]

1. John Bunyan, *The Holy War, Made by Shaddai upon Diabolus . . . Or, the Losing and Taking Again of the Town of Mansoul* (London: Nat. Ponder, 1696), 37–38; see *Works*, 3:268.
2. Bunyan, *The Holy War*, 39–40; see *Works*, 3:269.

King Shaddai decides that he will test Mansoul with an army of forty thousand soldiers led by four captains. (The marginal note in *The Holy War* says they are "the words of God.") Their names are Captain Boanerges, with a coat-of-arms of three burning thunderbolts; Captain Conviction, with a coat-of-arms of a flame of fire rising from the open book of the law; Captain Judgment, with a coat-of-arms of a fiery furnace; and Captain Execution, with a coat-of-arms of an ax at the root of a fruitless tree.[3] However, contrary to Diabolus' slander, these captains come not to destroy, but to break through the ice of Mansoul's proud defiance before Prince Emmanuel comes with the armies of faith, love, mercy, and grace to save Mansoul.

Bunyan's vivid story teaches us that Satan rules unchallenged over the souls of men until God in His mercy sends His Word. The Devil then hardens sinners against any kind of fear that would lead them to repentance and infects sinners with a hateful fear of God as if He were evil. What good will it do sinners, Bunyan said, if they fear God as the demons fear Him? Such fear will drive them away from God and His church, or at best clean up their lives a little while their hearts are still far from Him.[4] However, the preaching of God's Word begins to shake sinners with a sense of their sins, and this convicting work helps them to see their need for a Savior.

In order to understand what Bunyan was saying about fear in the life of an unbeliever, we must give our consideration to Bunyan's teaching—first, that sinners can fear God without loving Him, and second, that God can use the fear of hell and damnation to awaken sinners to serious consideration of the gospel.

The Ungodly Fear of God

When the Israelites trembled at the foot of Mount Sinai, Moses spoke these words to them: "Fear not: for God is come to prove

3. Bunyan, *The Holy War*, 41–42; see *Works*, 3:270.

4. John Bunyan, *A Treatise of the Fear of God* (London: N. Ponder, 1679), 174; see *Works*, 1:477.

you, and that his fear may be before your faces, that ye sin not" (Ex. 20:20). *Do not fear,* for God has come *so that you will fear.* From this apparent paradox, Bunyan deduced that God forbids some fear as ungodly, but commends another kind of fear.[5] This distinction proves to be crucial for Bunyan's theology, allowing him to differentiate unhealthy, sinful fear from the spiritually sound and fruitful fear of the Lord.

There is a kind of fear of God in the unconverted that Bunyan calls "ungodly fear." Bunyan was well aware that Scripture says of those still in a state of sin, "There is no fear of God before their eyes" (Rom. 3:18; cf. Ps. 36:1).[6] However, he interpreted this to mean that they have no godly fear that accompanies eternal life. The wicked may fear God in a wicked manner. Such fear can arise from "the light of nature," a phrase found throughout early modern writings to refer to the traces of the knowledge of God and His law remaining in the mind and conscience of fallen mankind (see Rom. 1:19–20, 32; 2:14–15; cf. Prov. 20:27). Even among pagans, Bunyan said, one can find people who are concerned to live reasonable and honest lives (see Gen. 20:9–11). Furthermore, the wicked may fear God in response to special acts of His providence, such as God's mighty works when He brought Israel out of Egypt.[7]

In his polemic against the inner-light teaching of the Quakers, Bunyan labored to distinguish between the natural light of conscience and the supernatural illumination of the Holy Spirit. Since Christ is the Creator of mankind, He gives to every man "light"—that is, the "conscience" that shows him there is an eternal God whose law opposes sin (see John 1:9; Rom. 1:20). This is an example of how nature itself teaches morality (see 1 Cor. 11:14).[8]

5. Bunyan, *A Treatise of the Fear of God*, 38–39; see *Works*, 1:446.

6. Bunyan, *A Treatise of the Fear of God*, 88; see *Works*, 1:457.

7. Bunyan, *A Treatise of the Fear of God*, 34–35; see *Works*, 1:445.

8. John Bunyan, *Some Gospel-Truths Opened* (London: J. Wright, 1656), 67–69; see *Works*, 2:151.

All men have this created or "natural" light, but not all men have the Spirit of Christ (see Jude 19). People may have a conscience that "does convict of sin," but they still follow false religions and continue to live as slaves of sin. The Holy Spirit, however, makes a person dead to sin and alive to righteousness (see Rom. 8:10). A guilty conscience by itself gives a person no more godliness than the demons have when they tremble at the prospect of God's punishing and tormenting them for their rebellion (see Matt. 8:29; James 2:19).[9]

Bunyan explained various ways that ungodly fear can show itself. His analysis is helpful for readers to discern whether their fear of God is godly or ungodly. First, men can fear God's judgment against their sins but, instead of repenting and submitting to God, can respond with resentment, anger, and hostility toward God. The Israelites exhibited this kind of ungodly fear in the wilderness when they accused God of seeking to destroy them.[10]

Second, ungodly fear can drive men away from God out of a sense of their sin and God's justice. Such was Adam's fear in the garden after he disobeyed God and the Israelites' fear at Mount Sinai when they saw God's majesty and heard His holy law.[11] Such ungodly fear engenders resentment and hardens the heart. Bunyan recognized this fear in many people in his day: "They cannot abide conviction for sin, and if at any time the Word of the law, by the preaching of the Word comes near them they will not abide that preacher, nor such kind of sermons anymore."[12]

Third, through ungodly fear, some people will participate in church to some extent but will refuse to seek God earnestly in personal prayer or to zealously serve His cause in the public arena. They are like the lazy servant in the parable of the talents, who

9. Bunyan, *Some Gospel-Truths Opened*, 70–72; see *Works*, 2:152.
10. Bunyan, *A Treatise of the Fear of God*, 36; see *Works*, 1:445.
11. Bunyan, *A Treatise of the Fear of God*, 37–38; see *Works*, 1:446.
12. Bunyan, *A Treatise of the Fear of God*, 39; see *Works*, 1:446.

feared his master as a hard, grasping man (see Matt. 25:24–25). In this case, fear makes a person view "Christ contrary to the goodness of his nature," and so it militates against any motion toward real godliness.[13]

Fourth, ungodly fear can motivate people to do works of the law in order to establish their own righteousness before God while rejecting Christ as their justification. Such were many Jews in Christ's time who were zealous for the law but would not trust in Christ as their righteousness. People who try to combine their works with those of Christ are like a man trying to sit on two stools.[14]

Fifth, ungodly fear can "put men upon adding to the revealed will of God, their own inventions and their own performances of them as a means to pacify the anger of God." Here Bunyan pointed to the Pharisees and to the Roman Catholics' practices of seeking peace with God by praying to Mary and engaging in self-flagellation.[15] Thus, like Adam and Eve in the garden after they ate the forbidden fruit, "awakened sinners" do not "think of Christ, or of the mercy of God in him for pardon, but presently they betake themselves to their own fig leaves, to their own inventions, or to the righteousness of the law, and look for healing from means which God did never provide for cure" (see Hos. 5:13).[16]

Bunyan's treatment of the ungodly fear of God displays a sensitivity to the potentially harmful effects of fear upon a person's soul and relationship with God. He was not an advocate for all kinds of religious fear, as if terrorizing people into outward religious acts were the goal. He knew by experience that it is possible to experience seasons of fear toward God without being a bit godly. As a child of nine or ten years, he had suffered "fearful dreams"

13. Bunyan, *A Treatise of the Fear of God*, 41–43; see *Works*, 1:447.

14. Bunyan, *A Treatise of the Fear of God*, 44–45; see *Works*, 1:447–48.

15. Bunyan, *A Treatise of the Fear of God*, 46–47; see *Works*, 1:448.

16. John Bunyan, *Exposition on the Ten First Chapters of Genesis, and Part of the Eleventh*, in *Works* (1692), 16; see *Works*, 2:432.

about devils and was sometimes troubled by "thoughts of the fearful torments of hell fire."[17] Nevertheless, he did not turn from sinning but instead became ringleader of a group of wicked youth. "In these days the thoughts of religion were very grievous to me; I could neither endure it myself, nor that any other should. So that when I have seen some read in those books that concerned Christian piety, it would be as it were a prison to me. Then I said unto God, 'Depart from me, for I desire not the knowledge of thy ways' (Job 21:14–15)."[18]

Fear That Is Godly for a Time

In addition to ungodly fear, Bunyan also taught that there is a kind of fear that serves a good purpose in driving a sinner to Christ, but after a person trusts in Christ it ceases to be helpful or appropriate. Whereas ungodly fear comes from remnants of the knowledge of God and His will in fallen men, stirred up by unusual providences, this fear is an effect of the Word and the Spirit. The "Word of wrath" is God's instrument to awaken a sinner to the fact that he has broken God's law and deserves eternal damnation. Bunyan calls this "godly" fear even though the sinner is not yet converted, because a sinner has just cause to fear, for he is in a state of sin and condemnation before God (see John 3:18, 36).[19] The law of God is instrumental in producing fear because "it is the chief, and most pure resemblance of the justice and holiness of the heavenly Majesty, and does hold forth to all men, the sharpness and keenness of his wrath."[20] Thus, in the allegory of *The Pilgrim's Progress*, Christian first appears "as a man clothed in rags," with a heavy burden on his back and a Book in his hand, and, "as he read, he

17. John Bunyan, *Grace Abounding to the Chief of Sinners*, 8th ed. (London: Nath. Ponder, 1692), 2–3; see *Works*, 1:6.

18. Bunyan, *Grace Abounding*, 5; see *Works*, 1:7.

19. Bunyan, *A Treatise of the Fear of God*, 48–50; see *Works*, 1:448.

20. John Bunyan, *The Resurrection of the Dead and Eternal Judgment* (London: Francis Smith, ca. 1665), 128–29; see *Works*, 2:114.

wept and trembled" and cried out, "What shall I do?"[21] This was Bunyan's personal experience as well.[22]

The law prepares the way for the gospel. Bunyan said, "If you would know the authority and power of the gospel, labor first to know the power and authority of the law. . . . That man that does not know the law, does not know indeed and in truth that he is a sinner; and that man that does not know he is a sinner, does not know savingly that there is a Savior."[23] Peter de Vries writes that, according to Bunyan, "It is not the intensity nor the duration of a conviction of guilt that matters. What matters is that we are aware of our sin to the extent that we come to realize we cannot do without Christ."[24]

Bunyan encountered this doctrine of conviction under the law being preparatory for faith in Christ by reading Luther on Galatians—the commentary that Bunyan so cherished in his own spiritual struggles. Luther said, "The true office of the law is to show unto us our sins, to make us guilty, to humble us, to kill us and to bring us down to hell, and finally to take from us all help, all succor, all comfort," yet not to lead to utter despair, "but that thereby they are prepared to come unto Christ."[25] However, Bunyan did not follow Luther in all things. Whereas Luther understood Paul's metaphor of the law as a schoolmaster (see Gal. 3:24) to refer to the moral law, Bunyan believed that the schoolmaster who leads to Christ is the ceremonial law—at least in Bunyan's early writings against the Quakers. In this interpretation of Galatians 3, he departs from the Reformation tradition.[26] However, Bunyan's understanding of a pre-conversion

21. John Bunyan, *The Pilgrim's Progress from This World, to That Which Is to Come*, 3rd ed. (London: Nath. Ponder, 1679), 1; see *Works*, 3:12.

22. See chapter 1 of this book.

23. John Bunyan, "The Epistle to the Reader," in *The Doctrine of the Law and Grace Unfolded* (London: M. Wright, 1659), A5r; see *Works*, 1:494.

24. Peter de Vries, *John Bunyan on the Order of Salvation*, trans. C. van Haaften (New York: Peter Lang, 1994), 138.

25. Luther, *Galatians*, fol. 171v, 172v [on Gal. 3:22, 23].

26. Richard L. Greaves, "John Bunyan and Covenant Thought in the Seventeenth Century," *Church History* 36, no. 2 (June 1967): 155–56. See Luther, *Galatians*, fol. 172r

experience of conviction of sin does follow the general teachings of Reformed theology as found in John Calvin and the Puritans.[27]

The fear of God's wrath is not merely the response of conscience but "is wrought in the heart by the Spirit of God."[28] The Holy Spirit convinces unbelievers of their sin and thus also of their state of damnation (see John 16:8–9). He does this especially through the law of God, "for by the law is the knowledge of sin" (Rom. 3:20). Bunyan quotes Romans 8:15, "For ye have not received the spirit of bondage again to fear; but ye have received the Spirit of adoption, whereby we cry, Abba, Father." The key word is "again," which Bunyan interpreted to indicate that the Spirit works first as the Spirit of bondage and then works as the Spirit of adoption—never again as a Spirit of bondage for believers in Christ. He is called "the spirit of bondage" because "he shows us that we indeed are in bondage to the law, the devil and death, and damnation" and imprisons men under a "sight and sense of our bondage-state" as long as He pleases.[29]

This is a supernatural work of God, an act of divine power through the Word. The Scriptures are the instrument, but only the power of God can break the heart. Bunyan wrote, "Now, when the hand of the Lord is with the Word, then 'tis mighty; 'tis mighty through God, to the pulling down of strongholds (2 Cor. 10:4). 'Tis sharp then, as a sword in the soul and spirit. It sticks like an arrow in the hearts of sinners, to the causing of the people to fall at his foot for mercy. Then 'tis, as was said before, as a fire, and as a hammer to break this rock in pieces."[30]

[on Gal. 3:23–24]; John Bunyan, *A Vindication of the Book Called, Some Gospel-Truths Opened* (London: Matthias Cowley, 1657), 17.

27. See Joel R. Beeke and Paul M. Smalley, *Prepared by Grace, for Grace: The Puritans on God's Ordinary Way of Leading Sinners to Christ* (Grand Rapids: Reformation Heritage Books, 2013).

28. Bunyan, *A Treatise of the Fear of God*, 50; see *Works*, 1:449.

29. Bunyan, *A Treatise of the Fear of God*, 50–52; see *Works*, 1:449.

30. John Bunyan, *The Acceptable Sacrifice: Or the Excellency of a Broken Heart* (London: George Larkin, 1689), 37; see *Works*, 1:694.

However, though supernatural, this work does not necessarily lead to salvation.[31] Such a work belongs to God's "common workings" in the soul as opposed to "a work that is saving and that will do the soul good to eternity." They may end not in salvation but in destruction for the person who, though afraid of damnation, still lacks "the grace of the fear of God" which accompanies true conversion.[32]

The Holy Spirit applies the law and the gospel to convict the soul to a depth and extent that sinners do not ordinarily experience when hearing the Word. Whereas the law by itself can inform the conscience of sinners to show them their gross violations of the commandments, the Spirit convicts sinners that all their righteousness, including their prayers, attending church services, and efforts at moral reformation, is but "filthy rags" (Isa. 64:6), utterly worthless before God (see Phil. 3:8)—"a bed too short to stretch yourself upon; and a covering too narrow to wrap yourself in" (see Isa. 28:20). The Spirit also uses the gospel to convince sinners of their wicked and damnable sin of unbelief toward Christ, of the necessity and sufficiency of Christ's righteousness to save sinners, and of the future coming of Jesus Christ to judge the world (see John 16:9–11).[33]

Spirit-worked fear is a significant aspect of Bunyan's biblical and experiential teaching on conversion. Without a profound sense of one's need for Christ and one's "lost condition without him," no one will come to Christ.[34] Bunyan saw this in many Scriptures. He coordinated the "spirit of bondage" in Romans 8:15 with what Paul described in Romans 7:9–10 as being "slain" by the law in his personal experience. Bunyan identified this experience with the period in Paul's life between Christ's appearing on the road to Damascus and

31. Bunyan, *The Acceptable Sacrifice*, 44; see *Works*, 1:695

32. John Bunyan, *A Holy Life, The Beauty of Christianity* (London: by B. W. for Benj. Alsop, 1684), 50–51, 63; see *Works*, 2:521–23.

33. Bunyan, *Some Gospel-Truths Opened*, 79, 83–86; see *Works*, 2:153–54.

34. John Bunyan, *Come, and Welcome, to Jesus Christ*, 4th ed. (London: by J. A. for John Harris, 1688), 22; see *Works*, 1:247.

Ananias's coming to Paul three days later with words of comfort and forgiveness (see Acts 9:1–18; cf. 22:12–16). Bunyan presented as further examples of this fear the cry of the Jews, "What shall we do?" after hearing Peter preach on Pentecost, and the cry of the Philippian jailer, "What must I do to be saved?" (Acts 2:37; 16:30).[35]

Bunyan placed this fear that prepares a sinner for salvation in Christ in the context of God's works of sovereign grace. Conviction of sin by the Word is "God's ordinarily dealing with sinners" when He comes in kindness and love to call them to salvation.[36] In *A Map Showing the Order and Causes of Salvation*, Bunyan outlined the God-initiated process leading to conversion in the following string of numbered circles:

1. Election, upon which stands;
2. The covenant of grace;
3. To the elect comes by the covenant effectual calling;
4. By which is given the Holy Ghost and the operations of it;
5. Which causes sound convictions for sin;
6. Whereat the soul is cast down;
7. Which occasions Satan to tempt to despair;
8. Which drives the soul to the promise;
9. Which strengthens faith;
10. Which encourages to pray;
11. Which causes God to hear;
12. And in mercy to reveal Christ's righteousness.

And as a result there comes confidence, true love for holiness, humility at the sight of sin, watchfulness against sin, patience under the cross, and more experience of God's goodness.[37]

35. Bunyan, *A Treatise of the Fear of God*, 51; see *Works*, 1:448–49.
36. Bunyan, *Saved by Grace*, in *Works* (1692), 566; see *Works*, 1:350.
37. Bunyan, *A Mapp Shewing the Order and Causes of Salvation and Damnation*, in *Works* (1692), no pagination, inserted before first page.

Bunyan's *Map* is an adaptation of the chart *A Survey or Table Declaring the Order of the Causes of Salvation and Damnation*, in which William Perkins also traces the steps of salvation flowing from God's electing love.[38] In effectual calling, Perkins placed between the preaching of the Word and faith the middle step of "mollifying" (softening) the heart. As Perkins explained in the accompanying treatise, *A Golden Chain*, this is the breaking of the heart with the hammers of the law of God, a knowledge of one's sinful nature and acts and the punishment that they deserve, a sense of God's wrath against sin, and a despairing of one's power to save himself.[39] Thus Bunyan stood in the Reformed experiential tradition in seeing conviction of sin as part of God's sovereign work to save sinners whom He had chosen in Christ.

This preparatory fear, Bunyan said, moves a man to "judge himself for sin" so that he falls down, broken, before God and acknowledges God's justice (see Ps. 51:1–4). It causes him to grieve and mourn over the misery of his spiritual condition (see Jer. 31:18–19). Casting aside any thoughts of deserving good or salvation, he waits upon God to see if there is hope (see Lam. 3:28–29). He humbly cries out for mercy to him, a sinner (see Luke 18:13). He will not receive comfort except from God's washing away his sins (see Ps. 51) and the Spirit's "coming to the soul with the sweet word of promise of life and salvation by Jesus Christ."[40]

However, not every person experiences the same process or degree of conviction of sin prior to faith in Christ. Bunyan communicated this variety of different people's experiences in *The Pilgrim's Progress*. Christian, on his way to the gate into the way of salvation,

38. Gordon Campbell, "The Source of Bunyan's *Mapp of Salvation*," *Journal of the Warburg and Courtauld Institutes* 44 (1981): 240–41. Perkins's chart was in turn derived from a chart by Theodore Beza (1519–1605), Calvin's successor at Geneva.

39. William Perkins, *A Golden Chaine, Or The Description of Theologie, Containing the Order of the Causes of Salvation and Damnation, According to God's Word* (London: John Legate, 1597), 141 [ch. 36].

40. Bunyan, *A Treatise of the Fear of God*, 53–54; see *Works*, 1:450.

fell into the Slough of Despond, a miry bog that nearly drowned him. Bunyan identified this as the "many fears, and doubts, and discouraging apprehensions" that come when "the sinner is awakened about his lost condition."[41] When Christian arrived at the gate, he knocked "more than once or twice," identifying himself as "a poor burdened sinner," and was brought in. The marginal note reads, "The gate will be opened to broken-hearted sinners."[42]

Another pilgrim, Faithful, also left home because he too realized that he lived in the City of Destruction, doomed by God to fire, just as Christian had.[43] Faithful later said that God's "work of grace in the soul" begins to show itself in "conviction of sin," especially the sinfulness of one's nature and the sin of unbelief (see John 16:8–9), which "works in him sorrow and shame of sin."[44] However, Faithful did not fall into the Slough of Despond—extreme spiritual depression—but instead was tempted by a woman named Wanton.[45]

As mentioned earlier, Bunyan also wrote a second part of *Pilgrim's Progress*, about Christian's wife, Christiana, after her husband died. Though she had formerly resisted Christian's religion, she had come to feel very guilty about her sins against her husband, and the memories of his cries, "What shall I do to be saved?" tore apart her heart.[46] When God's mercy to sinners was revealed to her, she followed him in the pilgrimage, accompanied by her children and a young woman named Mercy. They crossed the Slough of Despond without falling in, though Christiana almost slipped "and that not once nor twice."[47] When they came to the gate, they faced discouragements that Christian never did, such as the frightening sound of

41. Bunyan, *The Pilgrim's Progress*, 14; see *Works*, 3:92.
42. Bunyan, *The Pilgrim's Progress*, 31; see *Works*, 3:96.
43. Bunyan, *The Pilgrim's Progress*, 109; see *Works*, 3:117.
44. Bunyan, *The Pilgrim's Progress*, 137–38; see *Works*, 3:124.
45. Bunyan, *The Pilgrim's Progress*, 111; see *Works*, 3:117.
46. John Bunyan, *The Pilgrim's Progress, From This World to That Which Is to Come: The Second Part* (London: Nathaniel Ponder, 1684), 6–7; see *Works*, 3:173.
47. Bunyan, *The Pilgrim's Progress . . . The Second Part*, 21; see *Works*, 3:178.

a large, barking dog, but still were able to get in. The dog represents the Devil's discouragements to those who would pray for salvation.[48] Meanwhile, the girl named Mercy had to wait outside much longer, knocking (praying), before she too was welcomed in by the Lord.[49]

The different experiences of Christian, Faithful, Christiana, and Mercy exhibited Bunyan's belief that God leads people along different paths to conversion. Though all of them came under conviction of sin, fear of divine judgment, and a sense of the need for salvation, the degree and duration of their experiences varied. Bunyan taught by this that we can judge no one's experiences by a predetermined pattern of conversion. The Puritan Thomas Hooker (1586–1647) had similarly written that "all are not alike wounded for sin," for God gently pricks one person with a penknife, but pierces another with a sword.[50]

Though God's ways differ from person to person, it is His general method to awaken sinners to their need for a Savior before drawing them to Christ as their Savior. Have you experienced this? Has God's Spirit given you a taste of the bitterness of your sin? Do you see your sinful actions and heart as offensive to the holy God? Do you believe that you deserve to be condemned to hell? If you do not, then you can hardly look to Jesus Christ to save you from sin and damnation. Do not rest in a mere belief in Christ without a hunger and thirst for righteousness. Pray that God would show you who He is and what you are, and expose yourself to the heart-searching preaching of the Word.

When Good Fear Goes Bad

Bunyan believed that at the core of this fear of damnation was a "seed" that would continue and grow up into the godly fear that

48. Bunyan, *The Pilgrim's Progress . . . The Second Part*, 22; see *Works*, 3:179.

49. Bunyan, *The Pilgrim's Progress . . . The Second Part*, 24–25; see *Works*, 3:179–80. For a more detailed analysis of the pre-conversion experiences of Bunyan's characters, see Beeke and Smalley, *Prepared by Grace, for Grace*, 191–200.

50. Thomas Hooker, *The Soules Preparation for Christ* (The Netherlands: n.p., 1638), 155.

the children of God have toward their Father. By this *seed* he meant the humbling sense of God's majesty and holiness. However, once a person receives Christ by a living faith as the Spirit offers Him in the gospel, it is neither good nor godly to fear damnation and the wrath of God. The reason is that the person who has come to Christ by faith in the promise of God is forgiven of sin, placed in a state of "no condemnation" (Rom. 8:1), and "included in the covenant of grace," by which he may say that God is "my Father through Christ." God does not contradict Himself (see 2 Cor. 1:17–20), nor is a person "a child of God today, a child of hell tomorrow."[51]

Why then does a Christian sometimes experience fear of damnation even after trusting in Christ? Does not the experience of believers prove that a person can enjoy the Spirit of adoption but then come again under bondage? Bunyan did not deny the reality of this experience, but he counseled, "Let the Word be true, whatever your experience is."[52] According to His promise, "in his everlasting covenant of grace" that rests upon "the unchangeable purpose of God, and the efficacy of the obedience of Christ, whose blood also confirmed it," God will never remember the sins of His people again (see Heb. 8:10–12).[53] Bunyan appealed to the believer's union with Christ and the imputation of Christ's righteousness as the foundation of his security, writing, "I am united to Christ, and stand no more upon mine own legs, in mine own sins, or performances; but in his glorious righteousness before him, and before his Father; but he will not cast away a member of his body, of his flesh, and of his bones."[54]

Freedom from the fear of damnation hinges upon the doctrine that those who are truly converted will never fall away from God's

51. Bunyan, *A Treatise of the Fear of God*, 54–57; see *Works*, 1:450.

52. Bunyan, *A Treatise of the Fear of God*, 58; see *Works*, 1:450.

53. Bunyan, *A Treatise of the Fear of God*, 60–61 [irregular pagination, sig. E6v–E7r]; see *Works*, 1:451.

54. Bunyan, *A Treatise of the Fear of God*, 61 [irregular pagination, sig. E7r]; see *Works*, 1:451.

saving grace. Bunyan drew upon standard Puritan arguments for the perseverance and preservation of the saints. The Westminster Larger Catechism (1647) states,

> True believers, by reason of the unchangeable love of God (Jer. 31:3), and his decree and covenant to give them perseverance (2 Tim. 2:19; Heb. 13:20–21; 2 Sam. 23:5), their inseparable union with Christ (1 Cor. 1:8–9), his continual intercession for them (Heb. 7:25; Luke 22:32), and the Spirit and seed of God abiding in them (1 John 3:9; 2:27), can neither totally nor finally fall away from the state of grace (Jer. 32:40; John 10:28), but are kept by the power of God through faith unto salvation.[55]

John Owen employed similar arguments in *The Doctrine of the Saints' Perseverance Explained and Confirmed* (1654).[56]

The Holy Spirit does not bring believers in Christ into bondage to fears of damnation. The classic text on this topic, Romans 8:15, clearly presents an irreversible order to the Spirit's working: "For ye have not received the spirit of bondage again to fear; but ye have received the Spirit of adoption, whereby we cry, Abba, Father." Bunyan said that such bondage comes not from the Holy Spirit but from "the spirit of the devil." The Devil always does things out of order: he tries to persuade slaves of sin that they are sons of God, and, if someone is a child of God, then the Devil wants him to believe that he is a slave, for the Devil is a liar (see John 8:44).[57] When a believer sins, his heart will be troubled, and the Father

55. Westminster Larger Catechism (Q. 79), in *Reformed Confessions of the Sixteenth and Seventeenth Centuries in English Translation*, vol. 4, *1600–1693*, ed. James T. Dennison Jr. (Grand Rapids: Reformation Heritage Books, 2014), 4:315.

56. John Owen, *The Doctrine of the Saints' Perseverance Explained and Confirmed*, in *The Works of John Owen*, ed. William H. Goold (1850–1853; repr., Edinburgh, UK: Banner of Truth, 1965), vol. 11.

57. Bunyan, *A Treatise of the Fear of God*, 61–60 [irregular pagination, sig. E7v–E8r]; see *Works*, 1:451–52.

may discipline him, but "sin, after the Spirit of adoption is come, cannot dissolve the relation of Father and son" (see Ps. 89:30–33; Isa. 63:16–17; Gal. 4:4–7).[58] God's adoption is forever.

On the other hand, Bunyan warned that no one should "take courage to live loose lives, under a supposition that once in Christ, and ever in Christ." Such a conclusion shows that the person does not have the Spirit of adoption and is no child of God but remains under the power of the Devil.[59] Lest believers be tempted to backslide in this manner, Bunyan reminded them that, though the Father will never nullify His adoption of His children, He can take away their spiritual comfort and discipline them severely. In language that echoes *The Pilgrim's Progress*, he warns that "God can lay you in the dungeon in chains" and has sometimes so afflicted a believer that God "ran upon him like a giant" and "took him by the neck, and shook him to pieces" (see Job 16:14).[60] Christians should fear to sin against God. Even his "fatherly touch" is full of power, for He is not just an earthly father, but is the Father of glory with power over life and death.[61]

Yet Bunyan was deeply concerned that children of God never give way to fear God "as slaves fear a tyrant." Such a fear gives them "no strength against sin," but looking to God as one's Father in Christ promotes "a son-like bowing under the rod." It also encourages believers to come to God in prayer, to ask for a restoration of former mercies, and to hope that God's chastisements will lead to good in the end.[62]

Bunyan gave us a picture of a true Christian who was subject to slavish fear in Mr. Fearing, a character in the second part of *The Pilgrim's Progress.* Mr. Fearing constantly worried about whether

58. Bunyan, *A Treatise of the Fear of God*, 69–70; see *Works*, 1:453.
59. Bunyan, *A Treatise of the Fear of God*, 73; see *Works*, 1:454.
60. Bunyan, *A Treatise of the Fear of God*, 75, 78; see *Works*, 1:454–55.
61. Bunyan, *A Treatise of the Fear of God*, 85; see *Works*, 1:457.
62. Bunyan, *A Treatise of the Fear of God*, 83–84; see *Works*, 1:456.

he would make it to heaven. At the Slough of the Despond and the gate into the narrow way, he was held back by fear for many days. In fact, Bunyan said that he carried a kind of Slough of Despond in his mind wherever he went. Yet Mr. Fearing would not turn back, but pressed on. He actually had less trouble and fear about Hill Difficulty and the lions than others did, for his fears were about God's judgment, not earthly things. He loved the Valley of Humiliation and was outraged by Vanity Fair, which did not appeal to him at all. The Lord was especially tender and compassionate toward him, and God's ministers bore with him patiently. He was in fact a faithful and zealous Christian who denied himself many things and hated sin. He came safely through his pilgrimage to the heavenly city. However, his spiritual depression made his life a burden to himself and caused a lot of trouble for others.[63]

Bunyan's counsel is helpful for Christians today. If you are a believer in Jesus Christ and your faith is evident in a life of sincere though imperfect love and obedience, then you should not sink into a state of slavish fear toward God. Slavish fear is not from God's Spirit. God is your Father in Jesus Christ, and, though He will discipline you to make you holy, you should always look to Him as a child looks to a loving father. He does not discipline in wrath and rejection but in love and for our good. Fear to displease your Father, but never doubt His love. This is not the end of fear but the beginning of a new kind of fear, a childlike fear that the next chapters will explain.

63. Bunyan, *The Pilgrim's Progress . . . The Second Part*, 130–39; see *Works*, 3:212–15.

5

The Grace of Fear

Fear plays a crucial role in someone's becoming a Christian and living as a Christian. In the journey to the Celestial City depicted by Bunyan's *The Pilgrim's Progress*, Christian and his friend Hopeful meet a man named Ignorance, who thinks he will be justified and accepted by God for his good works. After separating from this deluded man, the two pilgrims begin to discuss true conversion. The question comes up as to whether people like Ignorance ever experience any conviction of sin or fear of judgment.

> *Christian*: Then, I say, sometimes (as I think) they may [have such convictions and fears], but they being naturally ignorant, understand not that such convictions tend to their good; and therefore they do desperately seek to stifle them, and presumptuously continue to flatter themselves in the way of their own hearts.
>
> *Hopeful*: I do believe, as you say, that fear tends much to men's good, and to make them right, at their beginning to go on pilgrimage.

Christian: Without all doubt, it does, if it be right; for so says the Word, "The fear of the Lord is the beginning of wisdom" (Job 28:28; Ps. 111:10; Prov. 1:7; 9:10).

Hopeful: How will you describe right fear?

Christian: True, or right fear is discovered by three things. 1) By its rise. It is caused by saving convictions of sin. 2) It drives the soul to lay fast hold of Christ for salvation. 3) It begets and continues in the soul a great reverence of God, his Word, and ways, keeping it tender, and making it afraid to turn from them, to the right hand or to the left, to anything that may dishonor God, break its peace, grieve the Spirit, or cause the enemy to speak reproachfully.[1]

As the last chapter showed, there are kinds of fear that are unhealthy and sinful, or that serve a good purpose only for a time in driving sinners to Christ. However, Bunyan also taught that there is a "godly fear" that continues in a believer's life all his days, for it is "the grace of fear."[2] It is unspeakably precious, "called God's treasure, for it is one of his choice jewels." Bunyan quoted Isaiah 33:6, "The fear of the LORD is his treasure."[3]

Bunyan anticipated an objection: "But the Scripture says, 'Perfect love casteth out fear'" (1 John 4:18). Therefore, how can it be good for people to continue to fear God after they have trusted in Christ and been adopted as God's children? Bunyan answered by saying that fear "may be taken several ways." There is the fear that devils and the damned have toward God, as well as the fear that the Spirit produces in driving sinners to seek salvation in Christ. However,

1. John Bunyan, *The Pilgrim's Progress from This World, to That Which Is to Come*, 3rd ed. (London: Nath. Ponder, 1679), 262–63; see *Works*, 3:159.

2. John Bunyan, *A Treatise of the Fear of God* (London: N. Ponder, 1679), 86; see *Works*, 1:457.

3. Bunyan, *A Treatise of the Fear of God*, 88; see *Works*, 1:457.

there is also the "son-like, gracious fear of God." This fear is not cast out by divine love. God's love casts out the fear that pertains to "torment" (1 John 4:18), the fear that anticipates God's wrath against His enemies. Godly fear is different, for it looks forward to God's blessing (see Eccl. 8:12), and it remains in God's children forever.[4]

This grace of fear makes a person excellent, beautiful, and honorable in God's sight—more so than any other quality. The Lord said to Satan in Job 1:8, "Hast thou considered my servant Job, that there is none like him in the earth, a perfect and an upright man, one that feareth God, and escheweth [turns away from] evil?" Bunyan calls the fear of the Lord "the salt of the covenant," which is necessary to season all that we are and all that we do (Lev. 2:13).[5] It is "the flower and beauty of every grace."[6]

The fear of the Lord is "the beginning of knowledge" (Prov. 1:7). The first saving revelation of God to the soul creates it, and it comes to life from the moment the soul receives God and Christ. The fear of the Lord is "the beginning of wisdom" (Ps. 111:10; see also Job 28:28). Only when a man comes to fear the Lord is he "truly spiritually wise," Bunyan said—wise in how to escape the spiritual and eternal ruin of sin and gain eternal life.[7]

The Bible also calls the fear of the Lord "a fountain of life" (Prov. 14:27). It "continually supplies the soul" with what a person needs to think holy thoughts and do what is right. Every motion of the fear of the Lord tends to produce spiritual and eternal happiness, just as water naturally makes things wet and the sun naturally shines with light (see Prov. 19:23).[8]

How does a person get this precious fear? Where does it come from?

4. Bunyan, *A Treatise of the Fear of God*, 158; see *Works*, 1:473.
5. Bunyan, *A Treatise of the Fear of God*, 89–90; see *Works*, 1:457–58.
6. Bunyan, *A Treatise of the Fear of God*, 160; see *Works*, 1:474.
7. Bunyan, *A Treatise of the Fear of God*, 91–92; see *Works*, 1:458.
8. Bunyan, *A Treatise of the Fear of God*, 94–95; see *Works*, 1:459.

Fear as a Gift of God's Saving Grace

Bunyan did not believe that godly fear is something that men can find within themselves and stir up or fan into flame. In line with the Augustinian and Reformed view of nature and grace, he taught that childlike reverence toward God is a grace that God must give to sinners through Jesus Christ. Bunyan wrote, "No man brings this grace into the world with him. Everyone by nature is destitute of it. . . . Men must have a mighty change of heart and life, or else they are strangers to this fear of God." Bunyan referred to the sweeping biblical condemnation of fallen mankind that Paul cites in Romans 3:18: "There is no fear of God before their eyes."[9]

The unconverted have many fears, but they do not fear God with a godly fear. Even to awaken them to a fear of damnation requires a mighty work of the Spirit—how much more a childlike desire to please God. Bunyan wrote,

> There is fear of man, fear of losing his favor, his love, his good-will, his help, his friendship. This is seen everywhere. How does the poor fear the rich, the weak fear the strong, and those that are threatened, them that threaten? But come now to God, why, none fears him, that is, by nature. None reverence him. They neither fear his frowns, nor seek his favor, nor inquire, how they may escape his revenging hand that is lifted up against their sins, and their souls because of sin.[10]

Godly fear can come only from God. Bunyan said, "It flows from the distinguishing love of God to his elect"—that is, "those that are wrapped up in the eternal or everlasting covenant of God." By "distinguishing love" he referred to God's special love

9. Bunyan, *A Treatise of the Fear of God*, 160; see *Works*, 1:474.

10. John Bunyan, *The Acceptable Sacrifice: Or the Excellency of a Broken Heart* (London: George Larkin, 1689), 118–19; see *Works*, 1:705.

that He freely set upon those sinners whom He chose. Bunyan quoted Jeremiah 32:40: "And I will make an everlasting covenant with them, that I will not turn away from them, to do them good; but I will put my fear in their hearts, that they shall not depart from me."[11]

Bunyan was a preacher of God's reigning and covenantal grace (see Rom. 6:14). By *grace* he meant "the free love of God in Christ to sinners, by virtue of the new covenant, in delivering them from the power of sin, from the curse and condemning power of the old covenant."[12] God's grace is "free and unchangeable" because it is based on an eternal covenant between God the Father and God the Son (see Ps. 89:3; Isa. 49:1–12; Zech. 9:9–11). The covenant revealed to the Hebrew patriarchs and their offspring was specifically made with one person, Jesus Christ (see Gal. 3:16–17). He is not a lowly creature like Adam, who fell in sin, but "the eternal Word of God," who is "as pure, as infinite, as powerful, as everlasting as God" (see Isa. 9:6; Heb. 1). The incarnate Christ alone fulfilled the condition of this covenant; it rested upon the work of one man (see Rom. 5:15–19).[13] Bunyan wrote, "God has said, Christ shall be the covenant of the people; that is, he shall be our conditions toward God."[14] Bunyan insisted that the covenant of grace was made with Christ alone, in order to place on the Mediator the full weight of responsibility for fulfilling its conditions.[15] This covenant embraced all the saved throughout history, and the coming

11. Bunyan, *A Treatise of the Fear of God*, 97; see *Works*, 1:459.

12. John Bunyan, *The Doctrine of the Law and Grace Unfolded* (London: M. Wright, 1659), 122; see *Works*, 1:494.

13. Bunyan, *Doctrine of the Law and Grace Unfolded*, 130–33; see *Works*, 1:522–23.

14. John Bunyan, *Justification by an Imputed Righteousness. Or, No Way to Heaven but by Jesus Christ*, in *Works* (1692), 99; see *Works*, 1:327. The original quote ended with the words "to God-ward" instead of "toward God."

15. Bunyan, *Doctrine of the Law and Grace Unfolded*, 137; John Bunyan, *Exposition on the Ten First Chapters of Genesis, and Part of the Eleventh*, in *Works* (1692), 67 [on Gen. 9:16]; see *Works*, 1:522; 2:492. However, Bunyan could also speak on occasion of "the covenant of grace which God has made with his elect in Christ" (*The Saints' Privilege and Profit*, in *Works* [1692], 260; see *Works*, 1:648).

of the new covenant (see Jer. 31:31–34; Heb. 8:8–10) was "a changing of the administration" of the covenant of grace, resulting in the abolition of the ceremonies that foreshadowed Christ (see Heb. 7–10) and a far clearer revelation of God's eternal covenant with Christ (see 2 Tim. 1:9–10).[16]

This idea of an eternal covenant between the Father and the Son can be traced back to the roots of Reformed theology, if not earlier, being found in the writings of the early Basel Reformer Johannes Oecolampadius (1482–1531).[17] Bunyan's view of the singular covenant in Christ has been compared to that of *The Marrow of Modern Divinity* (1645) and the Scottish Marrowmen of the eighteenth century.[18] Other theologians distinguished between the covenant of redemption (involving the Father and the Son) and the covenant of grace (involving God and man).[19] However, the idea of an eternal covenant between the persons of the triune God was commonly held by the Puritans. William Ames had said that the Father "ordained his Son to this office" of Savior by "a special covenant" stipulating that if Christ offered Himself as a sacrifice for sin, He would gain a spiritual "seed" or family (Isa. 53:10).[20] The Puritans, like Bunyan, saw Isaiah 49 as a "covenantal dialogue" between the Father and the Son about the work of salvation. One implication of this doctrine was that

16. Bunyan, *Doctrine of the Law and Grace Unfolded*, 138–40; see *Works*, 1:523–24.

17. Johannes Oecolampadius, *In Iesaiam Prophetam Hypomnematon* (Basle, 1525), 268b, cited in Joel R. Beeke and Mark Jones, *A Puritan Theology: Doctrine for Life* (Grand Rapids: Reformation Heritage Books, 2012), 239.

18. Richard L. Greaves, *John Bunyan*, Courtenay Studies in Reformation Theology 2 (Grand Rapids: Eerdmans, 1969), 104; Peter de Vries, *John Bunyan on the Order of Salvation*, trans. C. van Haaften (New York: Peter Lang, 1994), 105. See Edward Fisher, *The Marrow of Modern Divinity* (London: by R. W. for G. Calvert, 1645), 36–37. For a modern edition, see Edward Fisher, *The Marrow of Modern Divinity*, ed. Thomas Boston (Ross-shire, UK: Christian Focus Publications, 2009), 64–65.

19. De Vries, *John Bunyan on the Order of Salvation*, 102–5.

20. William Ames, *The Marrow of Sacred Divinity*, 1.19.4–5, in *The Workes of the Reverend and Faithfull Minister of Christ William Ames* (London: John Rothwell, 1643), 74 [pagination irregular, restarting in several places].

the Father had given particular people to Christ in order to save them, and so the Son will certainly accomplish their salvation and bring them to glory.[21]

Bunyan believed that salvation comes entirely from God's sovereign will in Christ. Sinners are saved by faith, and God works faith in no one except those who "before the world, were appointed to glory" (see Acts 13:48; Rom. 9:23).[22] Bunyan said that God determined "before the world began" that

- the price of the covenant from Christ would be His precious blood (see 1 Peter 1:19–20).
- the promise of the covenant to Christ would be "eternal life" (see Titus 1:2).
- the people blessed by the covenant in Christ were those chosen by God (see Eph. 1:4).[23]

God's "election" or choice of whom He would save is "free and permanent, being founded in grace and the unchangeable will of God" (see Rom. 11:5–6; 2 Tim. 2:19; Eph. 1:11)—a "decree" made "before the foundation of the world" (Eph. 1:4). Election is not based on any good thing foreseen in us, for God's election not only chooses the persons but also determines to give them everything necessary for salvation, so that the elect are God's new creation (see 2 Tim. 1:9; Eph. 2:10). Election is entirely in and through Christ (see Eph. 1:5–7), and therefore we must have faith in Christ in order to be saved (see 2 Thess. 2:13).[24]

The Lord is building a holy dwelling place for Himself out of a people elected before time began, redeemed by Christ's blood,

21. Beeke and Jones, *A Puritan Theology*, 246.

22. John Bunyan, *A Confession of My Faith, and A Reason of My Practice* (London: Francis Smith, 1672), 23–24; see *Works*, 2:598.

23. Bunyan, *Doctrine of the Law and Grace Unfolded*, 134–35; see *Works*, 1:522.

24. Bunyan, *A Confession of My Faith*, 25–30; see *Works*, 2:598–99.

and transformed by the Holy Spirit. Bunyan wrote in his poetic celebration of the church as the house of God,

> The builder's God, materials his elect;
> His Son's the rock, on which it is erect;
> The Scripture is his rule, plummet or line,
> Which gives proportion to this house divine;
> . . . .
> His compass, his decree; his hand's the Spirit
> By which he frames (what he means to inherit)
> A holy temple, which shall far excel
> That very place, where now the angels dwell.[25]

Though Bunyan's doctrine of election has its own peculiar features, it is clear that he was an heir of the Reformed experiential tradition in England. William Perkins, whose *Golden Chain* provided the basis of Bunyan's *Map* of salvation, had similarly taught, "Election is God's decree, whereby of his own free will he has ordained certain men to salvation, to the praise of the glory of his grace" (see Eph. 1:4–5). The "foundation" of the execution of this decree "is Jesus Christ, called of his Father from all eternity, to perform the office of the Mediator."[26]

The eternal purposes of the Father and the Son come to fruition in the individual's life by the work of the Spirit. Bunyan called the fear of God a *grace* because it is "a sweet and blessed work of the Spirit of grace, as he is given to the elect by God."[27] He cited Hebrews 12:28: "Wherefore we receiving a kingdom which cannot be moved, *let us have grace*, whereby we may serve God acceptably

25. John Bunyan, *A Discourse of the Building, Nature, Excellency, and Government of the House of God* (London: George Larkin, 1688), B1r–B1v; see *Works*, 2:578.

26. William Perkins, *A Golden Chaine, Or The Description of Theologie, Containing the Order of the Causes of Salvation and Damnation, According to God's Word* (London: John Legate, 1597), 34–35 [ch. 15].

27. Bunyan, *A Treatise of the Fear of God*, 87; see *Works*, 1:457.

with reverence and godly fear."[28] The Spirit of adoption is called "the Spirit of . . . the fear of the LORD" (Isa. 11:2) because He is "the author, animator, and maintainer" of a son-like fear toward the heavenly Father.[29] This Spirit was given to Jesus Christ in order that He would share the Spirit with His covenant seed, the church (see Isa. 59:20–21; Acts 2:32–33).[30] As a result, this Spirit-given reverence is "a dispensation of the grace of the gospel" through Jesus Christ, "a fruit of eternal love" flowing from the Father's heart; "it is only bestowed upon the elect, the heirs, and children of the promise, all others are destitute of it."[31]

The fear of the Lord is part of the new creation in Christ. It cannot come from the corrupt heart of fallen men, any more than grapes come from a thorn bush (see Luke 6:43–45). Bunyan said, "This fear flows from a new heart," which is "another fruit and effect of this everlasting covenant, and of this distinguishing love of God." Bunyan proved this by returning to the verse in Jeremiah that comes before the promise he quoted earlier: "And I will give them one heart, and one way, that they may fear me for ever, for the good of them, and of their children after them" (Jer. 32:39; see also Ezek. 11:19; 36:26).[32]

Whereas the spirit of bondage produces fear in those who are not yet saved, this saving fear is of another kind. Convictions of sin come from an illumination that reaches to the understanding and consciences of unbelievers, humbling them and perhaps resulting in some reformation of beliefs and behaviors; but conversion goes deeper, such that the power of God works upon their wills and

28. Instead of the KJV's "let us have grace," some other translations say something like "let us be grateful" (ESV) or "be thankful" (NIV). The Greek text reads "*echōmen charin*," an expression that could be rendered either way (cf. Luke 17:9; 2 Cor. 1:15). Bunyan did not read Greek, and he relied upon the English translations available to him.

29. Bunyan, *A Treatise of the Fear of God*, 87–88; see *Works*, 1:457.

30. John Bunyan, *Light for Them that Sit in Darkness: Or, A Discourse of Jesus Christ* (London: Francis Smith, 1675), 117; see *Works*, 1:420–21.

31. Bunyan, *A Treatise of the Fear of God*, 88–89; see *Works*, 1:457.

32. Bunyan, *A Treatise of the Fear of God*, 98–99; see *Works*, 1:459–60.

affections "to subdue them to the grace of the gospel."[33] The saving grace of fear is not merely an impression upon the mind but a transformation of the heart.

God looks with mercy upon the person who is broken under the fear of God. Psalm 51:17 says, "The sacrifices of God are a broken spirit: a broken and a contrite heart, O God, thou wilt not despise." However, Bunyan says, men's hearts are too proud, hard, and foolish to be broken of themselves. God must do it; a broken heart "is a sacrifice of his own providing."[34]

The presence of a childlike fear of God shows that a person is a child of God. Wherever the fear of the Lord is, there is spiritual life. Bunyan said, "This fear of the Lord is the pulse of the soul.... As long as the pulse beats, we count not that the man is dead."[35] He went so far as to say that if a person so much as desires to fear the Lord, it is a sign of saving grace (see Neh. 1:11). Mere desires for holy fear are not a high degree of grace but a low level of grace, and yet this is saving grace nevertheless.[36] Here again Bunyan follows the line of thought traced by Perkins, who taught that faith begins with a "hungering and thirsting after that grace, which is offered to him in Christ Jesus, as a man hungers and thirsts after meat and drink."[37] Such a desire for Christ and reconciliation with God Perkins called "a weak faith" but nonetheless "true saving faith."[38]

The great means by which God instills this fear in the heart is the Word of God (see Deut. 6:1–2; 31:12). The person who fears the Lord is the person who has obeyed the form of God's Word

33. John Bunyan, *A Holy Life, The Beauty of Christianity* (London: by B. W. for Benj. Alsop, 1684), 52, 54; see *Works*, 2:521.

34. Bunyan, *The Acceptable Sacrifice*, 146; see *Works*, 1:707.

35. Bunyan, *A Treatise of the Fear of God*, 226; see *Works*, 1:488.

36. Bunyan, *A Treatise of the Fear of God*, 227–28; see *Works*, 1:488.

37. Perkins, *A Golden Chaine*, 142 [ch. 36]. He explicitly identifies this hunger with the beginning of faith in William Perkins, *The Whole Treatise of the Cases of Conscience* (London: John Legat, 1606), 61 [1.5.3].

38. William Perkins, *An Exposition of the Symbole or Creed of the Apostles* (London: John Legat, 1595), 12.

"from the heart" (Rom. 6:17). "As a man drinks good doctrine into his soul, so he fears God." He is eager to learn the Word, and he stands in awe of it. But those who despise the teachings of God's Word, "they fear not God." Godly fear "flows from faith," for by faith in the Word of God, the godly are moved with fear to flee God's judgment and pursue His righteousness (see Heb. 11:7). Faith and fear hang together like "links of a chain."[39]

How does a Spirit-worked faith in the Word produce godly fear? As we saw earlier, Bunyan taught that God brings to life spiritual senses when He regenerates a sinner—senses by which he sees God, himself, and all things in a new light.[40] The soul now has "a blessed conviction" of God's knowledge of all the secret motives and thoughts of the heart, which inspires the fear of God (see 1 Kings 8:39–40). "A sense of the impartial judgment of God upon men according to their works" also creates holy fear (see 1 Peter 1:17).[41]

Faith pierces the soul with a sense of its sinfulness before God, producing godly sorrow and repentance and thus godly fear (see 2 Cor. 7:10–11). Faith also brings "a sense of the love and kindness of God"—that is, the "mercy of God by Jesus Christ." Without this sense of God's grace in Christ, there could be no childlike fear of God but only "wrath and despair," either a devilish fear of torment or a spirit of bondage. Bunyan quoted a classic text in this regard, Psalm 130:3–4:

> If thou, LORD, shouldest mark iniquities, O Lord, who shall stand?
> But there is forgiveness with thee, that thou mayest be feared.

Nothing binds the heart more powerfully to fear the Lord than hope in His mercy. The sense of God's grace creates "true tenderness

39. Bunyan, *A Treatise of the Fear of God*, 100–101; see *Works*, 1:460.

40. Bunyan, *The Acceptable Sacrifice*, 50–66; John Bunyan, *Christian Behaviour; Being the Fruits of True Christianity*, 3rd ed. (London: F. Smith, [1690]), 19–20; see *Works* 1:696–98; 2:552. See also the discussion in chapter 3.

41. Bunyan, *A Treatise of the Fear of God*, 106–7; see *Works*, 1:461–62.

of heart, true godly softness of spirit; this truly endears the affections to God," and this is "the very essence" of childlike fear.[42] Therefore, godly fear springs from a sense of God's saving love for sinners and is godly only insofar as fear is mingled with love for God. Childlike fear shows itself in a "tender love" for God's glory—especially for His Word, worship, and reputation among mankind.[43] Fear that "flows not from love to God" is "false fear," coerced by God's power.[44]

Do you have this grace of fear? Do you sense in your own heart a childlike reverence and love for God's majesty that reveals itself in a life of obedience? If not, then only Christ can give it by His Spirit. Repent and believe in the Lord Jesus. Use the means of grace, especially the regular hearing of preaching that opens the Bible and searches the heart. If you feel yourself becoming afraid of damnation, do not stifle this fear, but neither rest in it. Instead, let it drive you to cry out to Christ for salvation until you know He has saved you. If you do have this fear, then thank God for the supernatural gift of His grace. Turn Jeremiah 32:40 into your prayer for others: "Lord, do them good. Put Thy fear in their hearts, that they shall not depart from Thee." And cherish this holy fear as your best friend in this life and hope of glory in the life to come.

Why Christians Should Cherish Holy Fear

For those who fear God, Bunyan desired that, in this as in all graces, they would "do it more and more." Scripture exhorts believers in the same way in Psalm 34:9: "O fear the LORD, ye his saints: for there is no want [lack] to them that fear him." Every saint fears the Lord, but some are like Obadiah, who "feared the LORD greatly" (1 Kings 18:3). Christians should strive to be like Hananiah,

42. Bunyan, *A Treatise of the Fear of God*, 101–3; see *Works*, 1:460–61.
43. Bunyan, *A Treatise of the Fear of God*, 111; see *Works*, 1:462.
44. Bunyan, *A Treatise of the Fear of God*, 174; see *Works*, 1:477.

who was honored and given great responsibility because "he was a faithful man, and feared God above many" (Neh. 7:2).[45]

Bunyan presented many motives for Christians to grow in the fear of God. He reminded them that they received this grace of reverence as a gift of "God's distinguishing love to you." God has given them "his treasure, a choice jewel," given only "to those that are greatly beloved." Great gifts bring great obligations. If God has blessed you with this treasure, then you should "love it, nourish it, exercise it, use all means to cause it to increase and grow in your heart."[46]

Growing in the grace of fear keeps a Christian from many evils into which he might fall. Every God-fearing believer is the object of God's promise of perseverance: "they shall not depart from me" (Jer. 32:40). However, though a true Christian cannot totally and finally fall away, he may get himself into a lot of trouble by not pressing on to spiritual maturity. A healthy but careless child will often be tripping, falling, getting dirty—yes, even sometimes getting burns or almost drowning. Psalm 34:7 says, "The angel of the LORD encampeth round about them that fear him, and delivereth them." The fear of the Lord enables God's children "to depart from the snares of death" (Prov. 14:27), not just avoiding trouble, but also avoiding sin. Bunyan said that we cannot expect a watch to tell the right time if we never attend to its spring. The fear of the Lord is the spring (today we would say the battery) that keeps the Christian life in timely motion. Though there are many potential errors and extremes into which a religious person may fall, the fear of God can bring a Christian safely out of them all (see Eccl. 7:15–18).[47]

It is both wise and fitting for a Christian to fear the Lord greatly. Proverbs 14:16 says, "A wise man feareth, and departeth from evil." Bunyan noted, "It does not say a wise man has the grace of fear,

45. Bunyan, *A Treatise of the Fear of God*, 181; see *Works*, 1:478–79.

46. Bunyan, *A Treatise of the Fear of God*, 182–83; see *Works*, 1:479.

47. Bunyan, *A Treatise of the Fear of God*, 183–84, 195–96; see *Works*, 1:479, 482.

but a wise man *feareth*, that is, puts this grace into exercise."[48] If the fear of the Lord is a blessing, then isn't it wise to grow in the fear of the Lord? After all, it is only right and fitting to do so. If God is your Creator, shouldn't you fear Him? If God is King, is it not appropriate for His subjects to show Him reverence? If God is Father, shouldn't His children give Him honor and respect?[49]

The grace of fear does not degrade a human being into a wimp or a coward, but it cultivates a noble and courageous spirit. The fear of the Lord makes a woman excellent and honored (see Prov. 31:30). Christ coupled together fearing God and not fearing men (Luke 12:4–5). Bunyan said, "When I greatly fear my God, I am above the fear of all others, nor can anything in this world, be it never so terrible and dreadful, move me at all to fear them." If we do not want to fear the things that frighten most people, then Scripture counsels us to set apart the Lord as holy, "and let him be your fear, and let him be your dread" (Isa. 8:12–13). Bunyan, perhaps with *Foxe's Book of Martyrs* at his side, reminded us that if we look back to the jails, gallows, swords, and burning stakes by which God's people have suffered persecution, we will see that those who fear the Lord greatly have "the most mighty and invincible spirit that has been in the world."[50]

Though Christians suffer for their faithfulness, God honors those who honor Him, and he often does so in this life. The Lord chose the tribe of Levi for His ministers in the old covenant because they feared Him (see Mal. 2:4–6). It is God's order that men who fear God are to be put in positions of authority and responsibility (see Ex. 18:21; Neh. 7:2). To bless His people, God often entrusts power to men who fear Him, such as Joseph, Obadiah, Daniel, and Mordecai.[51] On judgment day, the Lord will remember those who

48. Bunyan, *A Treatise of the Fear of God*, 185; see *Works*, 1:480.
49. Bunyan, *A Treatise of the Fear of God*, 186; see *Works*, 1:480.
50. Bunyan, *A Treatise of the Fear of God*, 187; see *Works*, 1:480.
51. Bunyan, *A Treatise of the Fear of God*, 189–90; see *Works*, 1:480–81.

fear Him, sparing them as His dear children and cherishing them as His special treasure (see Mal. 3:16–17).[52]

If we desire to be useful to God in the home, church, or state, then we should cultivate the fear of the Lord. Ministers who walk in the fear of God are blessed by God to "turn many away from iniquity" (Mal. 2:5–6). Pastors who fear the Lord keep watch over themselves and their doctrine, saving themselves and their hearers (see 1 Tim. 4:16). Nor is this principle limited to those who hold an official position of leadership. Housewives whose chaste lifestyle is "coupled with fear" are the kind of women whom God uses to convict and convert ungodly husbands (1 Peter 3:1–2). Whether we consider husbands or wives, parents or children, bosses or employees, if they would join the fear of God to their lives, then they would "be made instruments in God's hands of much more good than they are." When unbelievers see Christians walking in the fear of the Lord, it tends to awaken their own consciences, but the lack of such reverent conduct in professing Christians is "a stumbling block to the blind."[53]

Bunyan said, "Thus you see what a weighty and great grace this grace of the holy fear of God is."[54] The benefits of having the fear of God, and exercising this grace more and more, are staggering. It is the flame that warms the whole life in holiness, the salt that makes all our works pleasing to God, and the light that reveals God's presence to the world. Christians should strive to grow in this precious grace more and more. Do you cherish the fear of the Lord?

52. Bunyan, *A Treatise of the Fear of God*, 197–98; see *Works*, 1:483.
53. Bunyan, *A Treatise of the Fear of God*, 193–94; see *Works*, 1:481–82.
54. Bunyan, *A Treatise of the Fear of God*, 107; see *Works*, 1:462.

6

Perfecting Holiness in the Fear of God

The Lord Jesus Christ warned people of their need to repent by telling a story about a fig tree (see Luke 13:6–9). Its owner came to it looking for fruit but found none. He said to one of his workers that for three years he had sought fruit from this tree but found nothing. He wanted it cut down. The worker, however, asked permission to tend it one more year and, if it still bore no fruit, then to cut it down. God is patient, but He is looking for fruit, or judgment will come.

In his exposition of this text, Bunyan asked, "What fruit does God expect?" The answer is "good fruit"—that is, "the fruits of the Spirit, the fruits of righteousness, which are by Jesus Christ" (see Gal. 5:22–23; Phil. 1:11).[1] These fruits include repentance and faith; they are the fruit of a holy fear of God. Bunyan wrote, "We should walk worthy of God; that is, so as we may show in every place that the presence of God is with us, his fear in us, and his majesty and

1. John Bunyan, *The Barren Fig-Tree, Or, The Doom and Downfal of the Fruitless Professor* (London: Jonathan Robinson, 1673), 47–48; see *Works*, 3:567.

authority upon our actions." Fruit that demonstrates "that his fear is in my heart" includes trusting and depending upon God, believing His Word, finding satisfaction in His presence, delighting in Him, thankfulness and worship, longing for heaven, generosity to the poor, exemplary conduct, patient endurance of trouble, and, in a word, *holiness*.[2] Bunyan said, "A man cannot love God, that loves not holiness."[3]

Though God declares believers righteous by faith alone, holiness is essential to salvation and eternal glory. Bunyan carefully distinguished the doctrine of justification by faith from the doctrine that good works demonstrate that a man is born again. He said,

> When I write of justification before God, from the dreadful curse of the law; then I must speak of nothing but grace, Christ, the promise, and faith: but when I speak of our justification before men, then I must join to these, good works. For grace, Christ, and faith are things invisible.... He then that would have forgiveness of sins, and so be delivered from the curse of God, must believe in the righteousness and blood of Christ: but he that would show to his neighbor that he has truly received this mercy of God, must do it by good works; for all things else to them, is but talk.[4]

The reason why justifying faith must produce good works is that faith receives Christ, and so the believer is in union with Christ by the Holy Spirit. Christ then dwells in the believer's heart by the Word and Spirit, and He transforms the character of the soul and the activity of the body.[5] In this teaching Bunyan followed Luther, who taught that by faith the Christian and Christ are "conjoined

2. Bunyan, *The Barren Fig-Tree*, 59–61; see *Works*, 3:569.
3. John Bunyan, *A Holy Life, The Beauty of Christianity* (London: by B. W. for Benj. Alsop, 1684), 46; see *Works*, 2:520.
4. Bunyan, introduction to *A Holy Life*, sig. A2r–A2v; see *Works*, 2:507.
5. Bunyan, introduction to *A Holy Life*, sig. A4r–A4v; see *Works*, 2:507.

and united together" so that Christ's righteousness is counted to the believer, the believer's sins have been counted against Christ, and Christ's victory and life now dwell in the believer so that faith is "not an idle quality" but powerful to produce good works.[6] As Bunyan said, "Faith is a principle of life . . . a principle of motion . . . a principle of strength, by which the soul opposes its lust, the devil, and this world, and overcomes them" (see 1 John 5:4–5).[7]

The necessity of faith for sanctification reminds us that holiness is by grace. Bunyan did not teach a perverse combination of justification by faith and sanctification by terror. He saw justifying faith as the engine that drives the believer forward into holiness. Reflecting on Titus 3:7–8, Bunyan said, "Good works do flow from faith." Furthermore, he asserted, "The best way to provoke both ourselves and others to this work, it is to be often affirming to others the doctrine of justification by grace, and to believe it ourselves." That is not to say that believing in justification automatically produces good works; rather, it provides the motivation and strength by which believers are careful to do good works and keep on doing them.[8]

Bunyan did not whip people toward holiness with terror, but he did teach sanctification by a holy fear of God. The fear of the Lord is an essential ingredient in the process of becoming more holy by grace. The apostle Paul wrote in 2 Corinthians 7:1, "Having therefore these promises, dearly beloved, let us cleanse ourselves from all filthiness of the flesh and spirit, perfecting holiness in the fear of God." Bunyan commented, "Where the fear of God in the heart of any is not growing, there no grace thrives, nor duty done as it should. . . . If then you would be perfect in holiness, if you would have every grace that God has put into your souls grow and flourish unto perfection, lay them, as I may say, to soak in this

6. Luther, *Galatians*, fol. 83r–83v.

7. John Bunyan, *Christian Behaviour; Being the Fruits of True Christianity,* 3rd ed. (London: F. Smith, [1690]), 15; see *Works*, 2:551.

8. Bunyan, *Christian Behaviour,* 12; see *Works*, 2:550.

grace of fear, and do all in the exercise of it."[9] Far from teaching legalism, this text makes clear that the fear of the Lord stands upon the promises of divine grace; this fear is produced by the Spirit, whom we receive by faith in Jesus Christ.[10] Godly fear and faith are not enemies but are sisters who work together to weave the garments of holiness.

Without the fear of God, Bunyan said, all obedience is mere hypocrisy, a deceptive mask. Ecclesiastes 12:13 says, "Fear God, and keep his commandments: for this is the whole duty of man." Bunyan concluded that holy fear "is that which sanctifies the whole duty of man."[11] He wrote, "It is a universal grace; it will stir up the soul unto all good duties. It is a fruitful grace, from it, where it is, flows abundance of excellent virtues, nor without it can there be anything good, or done well that is done."[12] Bunyan was no antinomian, but he affirmed the threefold use of the law that is taught in classic Reformation theology: the law convicts lost sinners, orders public society, and directs the lives of believers.[13] Obedience to God's commands as a rule of life for believers is possible only when they are motivated by the fear of the Lord.

What does the fear of the Lord look like? How does it influence a person to act?

The Form and Fruit of Godly Fear

Godly fear is a sense of reverence and awe toward God (see Ps. 89:7). This fear arises especially from a sense of God's holy majesty,

9. John Bunyan, *A Treatise of the Fear of God* (London: N. Ponder, 1679), 190–91; see *Works*, 1:481. "To soak" originally said "a-soak."

10. John Bunyan, *A Defence of the Doctrine of Justification, By Faith in Jesus Christ Shewing, True Gospel-Holiness Flows from Thence* (London: Francis Smith, 1673), 41; see *Works*, 2:299.

11. Bunyan, *A Treatise of the Fear of God*, 232–33; see *Works*, 1:491.

12. Bunyan, *A Treatise of the Fear of God*, 122; see *Works*, 1:465.

13. Anjov Ahenakaa, "Justification and the Christian Life in John Bunyan: A Vindication of Bunyan from the Charge of Antinomianism" (PhD Dissertation, Westminster Theological Seminary, Glenside, PA, 1997), 253–68.

as we have seen.[14] Bunyan said, "Nothing awes the soul that fears God, so much as does the glorious majesty of God." It also arises from a sense that God is not distant, but near and watching. As a result, the godly person says, "I stand in awe of him, he is my dread, he is my fear. I do all mine actions as in his presence, as in his sight. I reverence his holy and glorious majesty, doing all things as with fear and trembling before him."[15]

Fallen mankind by nature does not submit to God's law, nor is it able to do so (see Rom. 8:7). When God saves a sinner, God makes that person submissive (see Rom. 6:17). Bunyan wrote, "A broken heart is submissive; it falls before God and gives to him his glory." Thus such a heart is called a good and honest heart, "a heart fearing God."[16]

Bunyan said such reverence produces "tenderness of God's glory." It hurts the person who fears the Lord to see men dishonor the name of God (see Pss. 42:10; 119:136). Such a person longs for men to glorify God with both their mouths and their lives. This softness and zeal of heart moves men to take action for the honor of God's name. It provoked David to action when Goliath defied the armies of the living God (see 1 Sam. 17:26, 45). It strengthened Daniel and his three Hebrew brethren in Babylon to stand for the worship of the true God and Him alone, though wicked men threatened them with lions and fire (see Dan. 3:16–18; 6:10–16).[17]

The fear of God changes a man's moral tastes. Sin and vanity are the "sweet morsels" of a fool (see Job 20:12), but the fear of the Lord causes men to hate sin and turn away from it (see Prov. 3:7; 8:13; 16:6). That is not to say that the fear of God annihilates sin in the Christian, but where those "Canaanites" remain in the believer, "they are hated, loathed, abominated, fought against, prayed against,

14. See chapter 3 in this book.

15. Bunyan, *A Treatise of the Fear of God*, 108–9; see *Works*, 1:462.

16. John Bunyan, *The Acceptable Sacrifice: Or the Excellency of a Broken Heart* (London: George Larkin, 1689), 152–53; see *Works*, 1:710.

17. Bunyan, *A Treatise of the Fear of God*, 109–11; see *Works*, 1:462.

watched against, strove against, and mortified."[18] Bunyan offered several considerations to motivate people to depart from sin:

- God sees us when temptation comes.
- Sin brings great distress on those who embrace it.
- Christ suffered because of sin to save people from its power.
- Those now in hell are there because they loved sin and would not leave it.
- Claiming to be a Christian "is not worth a pin" if we do not repent of sin.
- A guilty conscience can make the day of our death very hard.
- On judgment day Christ will say, "Depart from Me," to those who do not depart from sin, but will bless and reward those who do.[19]

The believer's delight is no longer in sin but is now found in the law of God and in conforming his life to its commands. "Blessed is the man that feareth the LORD, that delighteth greatly in his commands" (Ps. 112:1). Sin and this world are no longer his masters, for he serves God and loves His law. Hypocrites and legalists may do some religious duties in a resentful manner or to gain men's praise, but the heart that fears the Lord has been opened and expanded with love for God, love for His holy people, and desire for the salvation of others. It acts with a free and royal spirit, given by the Spirit of the Lord.[20]

Godly fear also produces watchfulness. The godly keep watch over the heart, lest its deceits lead them to do wickedness (see Prov. 4:23). They watch and stand ready to resist the assaults of Satan (see 1 Peter. 5:8). They guard their mouths "as with a bit and bridle" because they know how easily the tongue of a man can be ignited

18. Bunyan, *A Treatise of the Fear of God*, 94; see *Works*, 1:458–59.
19. Bunyan, *A Holy Life*, 35–37; see *Works*, 2:518.
20. Bunyan, *A Treatise of the Fear of God*, 131–34; see *Works*, 1:467.

by hell to defile the whole body (see Ps. 39:1; James 3:2–7). They keep watch over all their conduct to stay in the "straight path" of obedience to Christ (Heb. 12:13). Godly fear does this by creating a sincere concern that a person never do anything to dishonor the name of God, to cause the saints to stumble, or give the enemies of God occasion to blaspheme.[21]

The fear of God moves people to pray fervently and regularly (see Acts 10:1–2). Bunyan exclaimed, "O prayerless man, you fear not God!" Indeed, without the fear of God, prayer is useless. Bunyan pointed his readers to Hebrews 5:7, which teaches that the Lord Jesus Christ Himself "was heard in that he feared." Filial or "son-like" fear is "essential to right prayer."[22]

Bunyan said that the fear of the Lord moves men to join with the assembly of God's people in Christian worship and fellowship. Gordon Wakefield observes that it is a mistake to read *The Pilgrim's Progress* as a commendation of individualism; "it is no lone journey," for "there are many good companions."[23] Those who fear the Lord speak often to each other in godly conference (see Mal. 3:16). All fear tends to move us to think about what we fear, even when we are trying not to think about it. Godly fear by its very nature moves a man's heart to think much and speak often about God, and that with reverence. Thus, the fear of the Lord makes Christian fellowship a time of holy conversation about the Lord and His ways.[24] It causes the church to engage in the holy ordinances of God's public worship with "great reverence of his majesty," for God has promised His special presence to their meetings, which become "his courts, and palaces." Godly people resolve to worship God in fear (see Ps. 5:7), for such worship is acceptable to God through Christ (see Heb.

21. Bunyan, *A Treatise of the Fear of God*, 111–12; see *Works*, 1:462–63.

22. Bunyan, *A Treatise of the Fear of God*, 122–23; see *Works*, 1:465.

23. Gordon S. Wakefield, "Bunyan and the Christian Life," in *John Bunyan: Conventicle and Parnassus; Tercentenary Essays*, ed. N. H. Keeble (Oxford: Clarendon Press, 1988), 124.

24. Bunyan, *A Treatise of the Fear of God*, 112–13; see *Works*, 1:463.

12:28). If it be offensive for a man to behave casually and lightly in the presence of his king, how much more must we serve God with proper reverence?[25]

Self-denial flows from holy reverence, as one denies oneself both those things that are contrary to God's law and those things that are lawful but not profitable at present. For example, Bunyan said, there was a precedent for governors in Judea to require a tax of food and money from the people, but Nehemiah did not do so "because of the fear of God" (Neh. 5:15). He did not demand his rights, because he was "tender of the honor of God, and of the salvation of his brother" and did not want to make the weak to stumble. In the same way, Paul would "eat no flesh while the world standeth, lest I make my brother to offend" (1 Cor. 8:13). Such God-fearing self-denial is a fundamental mark of a true disciple of Christ (see Matt. 10:37–38; Luke 14:26–27, 33).[26] The preeminent example of this self-denial is Abraham. How could Abraham "offer up his only and well-beloved Isaac" when God called him to do so? It is true that he did it "by faith" (Heb. 11:17). However, the Lord particularly commended Abraham's holy fear: "Now I know that thou fearest God, seeing thou hast not withheld thy son, thine only son from me" (Gen. 22:12). So Bunyan concludes that "there flows from this fear of God, a readiness or willingness, at God's call, to give up our best enjoyments"—even the things that are most precious to us on earth.[27]

Godly fear produces tenderhearted compassion to saints who are in need and distress. Bunyan held up the example of Obadiah—not the prophet, but the civil servant in Ahab's regime. When wicked Queen Jezebel sought to kill the prophets of the Lord, Obadiah hid a hundred of them in a cave and provided them with food and water because he "feared the Lord greatly" (1 Kings 18:3–4). In a

25. Bunyan, *A Treatise of the Fear of God*, 114–15; see *Works*, 1:463.
26. Bunyan, *A Treatise of the Fear of God*, 115–17; see *Works*, 1:463–64.
27. Bunyan, *A Treatise of the Fear of God*, 123–24; see *Works*, 1:465.

time of fierce persecution, this God-fearing man protected God's servants "even under Jezebel's nose," risking his own life to show mercy to his brothers.[28]

The fear of God delivers us from the duplicity of being religious simply to win man's praise or reward, and it moves us to serve God with sincerity. Bunyan quoted Colossians 3:22, that we must do our work "not with eyeservice, as menpleasers; but in singleness of heart, fearing God." Godly fear is the mortal enemy of hypocrisy in our souls because, Bunyan said, the "grace of fear of God retains and keeps upon the heart a reverent and awful sense of the dread majesty and all-seeing eye of God, also a due consideration of the day of account before him; it likewise makes his service sweet and pleasing, and fortifies the soul against all discouragements."[29]

Godly fear is also the antidote to spiritual pride: "Be not high-minded, but fear" (Rom. 11:20). Pride is a deadly, soul-damning sin; it cast the devils down and condemned them to hell (see 1 Tim. 3:6). Pride causes you to forget "what you are by nature," so that you grow puffed up about your abilities and do not remember "the need that you have of continual pardon, support, and supplies from the Spirit of grace." But, Bunyan wrote, the fear of God "will make you little in our own eyes, keep you humble, put you upon crying to God for protection, and upon lying at his foot for mercy." The fear of the Lord turns a man away from trusting in himself and makes him desire counsel and instruction from God. It "makes a man walk lowly, softly, and so securely in the way."[30] Humility enables each person also to live well according to his place in society. (Bunyan was not a social revolutionary.) He said, "It is amiable [lovely] and pleasant to God, when Christians keep their rank, relation, and station, doing all as become their quality and calling." When Christians focus on doing the work that properly belongs to their position and relationships

28. Bunyan, *A Treatise of the Fear of God*, 120–22; see *Works*, 1:464–65.
29. Bunyan, *A Treatise of the Fear of God*, 118–19; see *Works*, 1:464.
30. Bunyan, *A Treatise of the Fear of God*, 125–27; see *Works*, 1:467–68.

in the household and society, "then they are like the flowers in the garden, that stand and grow where the Gardener has planted them."[31]

Fear leads to hope. Bunyan observed that Psalm 147:11 says, "The LORD taketh pleasure in them that fear him, in those that hope in his mercy." The parallel between fearing God and hoping in His mercy implies that "they be the men that fear the Lord, even they that hope in his mercy; for true fear produces hope in God's mercy." How is this so? Bunyan outlines it in stages. First, the fear of God moves the heart to seriously seek after God's appointed way of salvation. It gives the sinner a "special regard to the Word" as the place where God has revealed this salvation. Then godly fear moves him to submit himself to God's way. The same fear "carries in it self-evidence" of saving grace, and as a result hope blossoms into assurance of salvation, for God takes pleasure in those who fear Him.[32] Furthermore, godly fear shows itself in "a reverent use of the means" of grace by which we grow in holiness. There is such a thing as counterfeit faith, leading to counterfeit hope—that is, a hope without any pursuit of holiness (see Heb. 12:14). The fear of God moves believers to work out their salvation (see Phil. 2:12), not to merit eternal life but to lay hold of it (see 1 Tim. 6:11–12). In this way, godly fear validates the reality of their hope that they are saved and will be saved forever.[33]

How to Grow in the Fear of the Lord

Just as the New Testament teaches us that Christian repentance requires both putting off sin and putting on righteousness (see Eph. 4:22–24), so Bunyan taught that to grow in the fear of God, the believer must both cease from the things that hinder it and do the things that help it. The pursuit of holiness requires effort because "the heart of a Christian is a heart subject to bring forth

31. John Bunyan, "Epistle to the Reader," in *Christian Behaviour*, sig. A4r–A4v; see *Works*, 2:550.

32. Bunyan, *A Treatise of the Fear of God*, 127–28; see *Works*, 1:466.

33. Bunyan, *A Treatise of the Fear of God*, 129–30; see *Works*, 1:466–67.

weeds," Bunyan said. Just as the Holy Spirit is always producing good things in the heart, so the flesh is always producing evil (see Gal. 5:17). Hence the Bible is full of warnings to believers to keep watch over their hearts and lives. It is far too easy to sin and to become confused about what is right in God's sight.[34]

A great enemy of the fear of God is a hardened heart (see Isa. 63:17). Beware of "the beginnings of sin," for, as David's life shows, one lustful glance can lead to adultery and murder. Be quick to repent of sin, for continuing in sin hardens the heart.[35] Remember that Satan is like the person who wants to split a block of wood; he puts the thin end of the wedge in first and then drives further and splits the wood wider.[36] Bunyan identified some sins in particular that are opposed to the fear of the Lord:

- *A light and wanton heart*, on which God's holiness and judgments rest lightly, but whose affections are quick to run to spiritual adultery with the world (see Jer. 3:8).
- *A covetous heart*, ruled by desires for earthly riches and gain and diametrically opposed to the fear and love of God (see Ex. 18:21; 1 John 2:15).
- *An unbelieving heart*, which makes God, heaven, and hell seem distant and unreal to the soul, and so is the source of all evil (see Heb. 3:12).
- *A forgetful heart*, which leads to a tendency to overlook God's kindness and patience, on the one hand, and on the other hand to ignore His judgments on the earth (see Job 21:6; 23:15–16).
- *A proud and complaining heart*, which finds fault with God's ways and would correct Him with "superior" wisdom instead of meekly waiting under God's hand (see Ps. 39:9).

34. Bunyan, *Christian Behaviour*, 25–26; see *Works*, 2:553.
35. Bunyan, *A Treatise of the Fear of God*, 210–11; see *Works*, 1:486.
36. Bunyan, *The Acceptable Sacrifice*, 178; see *Works*, 1:713.

- *An envious heart*, which takes the place of "a controller and a judge" to lay claim self-righteously to what God gave someone else, or to envy sinners who appear to prosper (see Prov. 23:17).
- *An undisciplined heart*, which will not apply itself to the practice of spiritual disciplines such as prayer, giving to the poor, self-denial, and so on.[37]

When such sins arise within the believer's soul, he must repent of them quickly and strive to put them to death, or they will harden his heart against the fear of the Lord.

In order to pursue the fear of God, we must learn to distinguish godly fear from ungodly fear. Christians must be on their guard lest a kind of fear grow in them that God counts as His enemy and is damaging to His people. They must obey God's many commands to "fear not" by putting off ungodly fear (see Gen. 15:1; 26:24; 46:3; Ex. 14:13; 20:20; Num. 14:9; 21:34; Isa. 41:10, 13–14; 43:1; 44:2, 8; 54:4; Jer. 30:10; Dan. 10:12, 19; Joel 2:21; Hag. 2:5; Zech. 8:13).[38]

Believers must also learn to rightly distinguish childlike fear from spiritual bondage (see Rom. 8:15; 2 Tim. 1:7). Once a person comes to saving faith in Jesus Christ, a fearful experience of bondage is not from the Holy Spirit but from the Devil, and it motivates a person to live not like a son of God but like a slave. Christians should conscientiously resist slavish fear, for it "nourishes unbelief," Bunyan wrote.[39] This is one reason why he spent so much time in his *Treatise of the Fear of God* in describing the spirit of bondage.[40]

Bunyan said that those who desire to grow in the grace of godly fear should implement the following spiritual disciplines. They should study to "grow in the knowledge of the new covenant." The covenant of grace is designed both to put down ungodly fear and to

37. Bunyan, *A Treatise of the Fear of God*, 212–17; see *Works*, 1:486–87.
38. Bunyan, *A Treatise of the Fear of God*, 198–99; see *Works*, 1:483.
39. Bunyan, *A Treatise of the Fear of God*, 199–201; see *Works*, 1:483.
40. See the latter portions of chapter 4 in this book.

promote true holiness (see Luke 1:69–75). It reveals "the complete salvation of your soul" through "the blood of the Son of God." Therefore, "the knowledge and faith of this covenant is of absolute necessity to bring us into this liberty, and out of our slavish terrors, and so, consequently, to cause us to grow in that son-like, godly fear," which was fitting even for the Son of God Himself.[41]

Christians should exercise their faith strongly in order to walk in assurance of salvation. Bunyan spoke of guarding your "evidences for heaven," which he explained as the exercises of a living faith in Jesus Christ (see Ps. 61:2–5).[42] Elsewhere, he spoke of the "self-evidence" of salvation that is found in fear of God (see Ps. 147:11) and love of the brethren (see 1 John 3:14).[43] Holiness and good works do not merit or earn eternal life, but a saving hope in Christ is evident in the way that it purifies the heart and prepares the soul for glory. Thus a Christian makes his calling and election sure by walking in growing practical godliness (see 2 Peter 1:5–11).[44] Bunyan was using the Puritan methods of establishing assurance upon both faith in the promises and a Spirit-given sight of saving grace in your inward life and outward conduct.[45]

However, Bunyan also taught that sometimes a believer may lose sight of God's sanctifying grace in his soul by a spiritual lapse, just as Christian in *The Pilgrim's Progress* lost his roll (a symbol of assurance of salvation) for a time.[46] Bunyan wrote, "Our evidences, which declare that we have a right to the eternal inheritance, are often out of our own hand." When this happens, the believer must look again to Christ our Advocate to restore to him the joy of salvation, for Christ

41. Bunyan, *A Treatise of the Fear of God*, 202–3; see *Works*, 1:484.

42. Bunyan, *A Treatise of the Fear of God*, 203–5; see *Works*, 1:484.

43. Bunyan, *A Treatise of the Fear of God*, 128; see *Works*, 1:466.

44. Bunyan, *A Treatise of the Fear of God*, 130–31; see *Works*, 1:467.

45. The Puritans based assurance first upon the promises, and then upon the godly motions of the soul (the mystical syllogism) and practical Christian obedience (the practical syllogism). See Joel R. Beeke, *The Quest for Full Assurance: The Legacy of Calvin and His Successors* (Edinburgh, UK: Banner of Truth, 1999), 65–72, 132–41.

46. John Bunyan, *The Pilgrim's Progress from This World, to That Which Is to Come*, 3rd ed. (London: Nath. Ponder, 1679), 63; see *Works*, 3:105.

alone answered God's justice and is our righteousness (see Ps. 51:12; 1 John 2:1–2).[47] However, it is not a head knowledge of the promises of God's covenant, but a regular hiding of oneself in Christ by faith in the promises, that quiets ungodly fears and strengthens godly fear. The goodness of God promotes holy fear (see Hos. 3:5), and so Bunyan said, "Be much in the faith of the promise"—the promise that shows you that God has given you Christ, and with Him all good things.[48] The more you know His goodness, the more you fear Him. Meditating on Christ's death on the cross for your sins also "will dissolve your heart into tears, and make it soft and tender."[49]

Exercise faith not only in the grace of God but also in the majesty of God. Think often of God's greatness. Bunyan said, "If we would fear him more, we must abide more in the sense and faith of his glorious majesty." Meditating on God will produce a "holy and awful dread and reverence of his majesty," for His very name is glorious and fearsome (see Deut. 28:58).[50] He wrote, "Labor after a deep knowledge of God" and "keep it warm upon your heart," including the knowledge of His presence everywhere, His "piercing eye" that sees all things, His power to destroy the entire universe, His justice like a consuming fire, and His faithfulness to keep both His promises and His threats.[51] Remember the judgments of God—both the judgment of destruction on hypocrites and the judgments of correction on careless Christians. He is not a God to be trifled with.[52]

The heart also grows in fear and contrition by increasing in the knowledge of sin. Bunyan said, "Labor to get, and keep a deep sense of sin in its evil nature, and in its soul-destroying effects upon your heart. Be persuaded that it is the only enemy of God."

47. John Bunyan, *The Work of Jesus Christ as an Advocate* (London: Dorman Newman, 1688), 147–49; see *Works* 1:188.

48. Bunyan, *A Treatise of the Fear of God*, 206; see *Works*, 1:485.

49. Bunyan, *A Treatise of the Fear of God*, 211; see *Works*, 1:486.

50. Bunyan, *A Treatise of the Fear of God*, 205–6; see *Works*, 1:484–85.

51. Bunyan, *The Acceptable Sacrifice*, 180–81; see *Works*, 1:713.

52. Bunyan, *A Treatise of the Fear of God*, 207; see *Works*, 1:485.

Sin turned angels into devils and cast them into hell (see 2 Peter 2:4; Jude 6). Sin cast Adam out of paradise, drowned the ancient world, and brought fire on Sodom and Gomorrah. Sin "cost Christ his blood to redeem you from the curse it has brought upon you." And if anything keeps a person out of heaven, it will be sin.[53]

The means by which to do all these things is the Word of God. The Holy Scriptures should always be before our eyes, always sounding in our ears, and always stirring thoughts and affections in our hearts. Bunyan said, "Every grace is nourished by the Word" (see Prov. 4:20–22). The Christian should not treat the Word as mere information, however, or as simply a help for spiritual growth, but should always remember from whom it comes. It is the Word of One who is both the "mighty and glorious God" and the loving and compassionate Father of His children.[54]

Bunyan specifically called upon heads of households to take up their responsibilities to bring the Word to their families and their families to the Word. The head of each household should "diligently and frequently" teach the Bible to his family, making suitable applications to each particular person and situation (see Gen. 18:19; Josh. 24:15).[55] The father (or the mother, if he is not able) must not neglect the duty of leading family worship, "reading the Word and prayer" as a family.[56] He must tell them about man's fallen state, sin, death, hell, the crucified Savior, and the promise of life to all who believe.[57] He must also bring them to "God's public worship" so that "God may convert their souls," or, if they absolutely refuse, he should bring godly preachers to his home.[58] He should govern his home as one who fears God, and, though only God can rule the heart, he should expect his children in the home to obey the Scriptures in

53. Bunyan, *The Acceptable Sacrifice*, 181–82; see *Works*, 1:713.
54. Bunyan, *A Treatise of the Fear of God*, 206; see *Works*, 1:485.
55. Bunyan, *Christian Behaviour*, 39–40; see *Works*, 2:555.
56. Bunyan, *Christian Behaviour*, 44; see *Works*, 2:556.
57. Bunyan, *Christian Behaviour*, 56; see *Works*, 2:556.
58. Bunyan, *Christian Behaviour*, 42–43; see *Works*, 2:556.

their outward behavior. Yet his goal should always be the glory of God, as he should patiently absorb personal injuries in love but zealously oppose all open rebellion against the Lord. He must not be like those insane people who rage at every personal offense but laugh, or at least fail to rebuke, when God's holy name is dishonored.[59] Instead, he should conduct himself in a way that shows that the things he teachesthem are "not fables, but realities"—realities a thousand times more important than earthly things. He must live such a holy life that when his children think of God, they will, like Jacob, remember that the Lord was the fear of their father (see Gen. 31:53).[60]

Reading and hearing the Word must be joined with much prayer. Turn Psalm 86:11 into your personal and frequent request to God: *unite my heart to fear Thy name*. Believers can pray this with confidence, Bunyan said, because "to fear God is that which is according to his will, and 'if we ask any thing according to his will, he heareth us'" (1 John 5:14).[61] He wrote, "Prayer is as the pitcher that fetches water from the brook." Thus he said, "See you a man that prays but a little? That man fears God but little, for it is the praying soul, the man that is mighty in praying, that has an heart for the fear of God to grow in."[62]

Christians must not seek to grow in the fear of God in a half-hearted manner. The world mocks at the fear of God, thinking it a weakness, a symptom of an unhealthy mind. Christians, however, should not be ashamed of the fear of the Lord. Bunyan called the believer to "devote" himself to the fear of the Lord, even to "addict yourself to it" with habitual dedication. Find your peace and joy in meditating on God and showing reverence to His name and Word and worship. "Then," Bunyan said, "will you fear, and grow in this grace of fear."[63]

59. Bunyan, *Christian Behaviour*, 48–49; see *Works*, 2:556.
60. Bunyan, *Christian Behaviour*, 56–57; see *Works*, 2:556.
61. Bunyan, *A Treatise of the Fear of God*, 209; see *Works*, 1:485.
62. Bunyan, *A Treatise of the Fear of God*, 212; see *Works*, 1:486.
63. Bunyan, *A Treatise of the Fear of God*, 209; see *Works*, 1:485.

7

Trembling at the Word

In Bunyan's most famous story, the pilgrim begins his journey with "a book in his hand, and a great burden upon his back." The journey ends with Hopeful helping Christian to struggle through the river of death by saying, "My brother, you have quite forgot the text," and quoting Scripture.[1] From beginning to end, Bunyan's vision of the Christian life revolved around the Bible. Without the Bible, the Christian can be neither fearful nor fearless in a godly way.

The Holy Scriptures are so closely connected to godly fear that they are actually called "the fear of the LORD" in Psalm 19:9, as a comparison with the preceding verses shows.[2] The Word of God is both "the object of a Christian's fear" and "the rule and director of our fear," because "we know not how to fear the Lord in a saving way without its guidance and direction."[3] The Word was given so that we might learn the fear of the Lord (see Deut. 6:1–3, 24).

1. John Bunyan, *The Pilgrim's Progress from This World, to That Which Is to Come*, 3rd ed. (London: Nath. Ponder, 1679), 1, 275; see *Works*, 3:12, 163–64.

2. John Bunyan, *A Treatise of the Fear of God* (London: N. Ponder, 1679), 22; see *Works*, 1:442.

3. Bunyan, *A Treatise of the Fear of God*, 22–23; see *Works*, 1:442–43.

Those who tremble at God's Word receive God's grace (see 2 Chron. 34:26–27; Ezra 9:4; 10:3; Isa. 66:2, 5).[4] Regardless of what powerful men may say or do, the heart of the godly stands in awe of God's Word (see Ps. 119:161).[5] What makes the Bible a book of holy fear? How should that affect the way that Christians read and preach it?

The Voice of the Lord Is Full of Majesty

What makes the Bible a fearful book? God is the author of the Scriptures. Bunyan received the Bible not as the words of men but as the Word of God. The prophets and apostles "have spoken by divine inspiration."[6] Bunyan wrote, "All the Holy Scriptures are the words of God" (see 2 Tim. 3:16; 2 Peter 1:21).[7] The Bible resounds with the declaration, "Thus saith the Lord." Therefore, God's own majesty thunders in His Word. Bunyan wrote, in a mighty rush of biblical texts, "The word of a king is as the roaring of a lion; where the word of a king is, there is power; what is it then when God, the great God shall roar out of Zion, and utter his voice from Jerusalem, whose voice shakes not only earth, but also heaven. . . . The voice of the Lord is powerful, the voice of the Lord is full of majesty" (see Prov. 19:12; Eccl. 8:4; Joel 3:16; Ps. 29:4).[8] To those who wish that God would speak to them directly, Bunyan said that the Scriptures "are the truth as really as if God should speak to you from heaven through the clouds."[9]

The majesty of Scripture shines in its truthfulness and inerrancy. Bunyan said, "It is to be called a fearful Word, because of the truth and faithfulness of it." Christ taught that the Scriptures cannot be broken (see John 10:35). They are "the Scripture of truth" and "the

4. Bunyan, *A Treatise of the Fear of God*, 24–26; see *Works*, 1:443.

5. Bunyan, *A Treatise of the Fear of God*, 109; see *Works*, 1:462.

6. John Bunyan, *A Few Sighs from Hell, Or, The Groans of a Damned Soul* (London: by Ralph Wood, for M. Wright, 1658), 139; see *Works*, 3:707.

7. John Bunyan, *A Confession of My Faith, and A Reason of My Practice* (London: Francis Smith, 1672), 43; see *Works*, 2:601.

8. Bunyan, *A Treatise of the Fear of God*, 26–27; see *Works*, 1:443.

9. Bunyan, *A Few Sighs from Hell*, 202; see *Works*, 3:720.

true sayings of God" (Dan. 10:21; Rev. 19:9). The least part of a single letter of the Holy Scriptures is more enduring than heaven and earth (see Ps. 119:89; Matt. 5:18; 24:35).[10] The Scriptures are trustworthy in all that they say. Bunyan said, "They cannot be broken, but will certainly be fulfilled in all the prophecies, threatenings, and promises, either to the salvation or damnation of men" (see John 10:35; Gal. 3:8; Acts 13:40–41).[11] He would not submit his conscience to the judgments of mere men but would "be judged by the Scriptures; I am sure that is infallible, and cannot err."[12] He said, "They are the words of God, and therefore I cannot err in quoting of them."[13] The apostles were "endued with the Holy Ghost" so that "they, as to their doctrine, were infallible, it was impossible they should err; he that despised their doctrine, despised God himself."[14]

The Word of God is its own evidence and authentication, for no authority can be higher than God. Bunyan said, "True faith carries along with it an evidence of the certainty of what it believes; and that evidence is the infallible Word of God." Faith believes in God and in Christ as the only way to God because "the Word of God does say so." Saving faith is therefore no weak thing but is powerful to move people. "Faith is grounded upon the voice of God in the Word."[15]

The Bible is the only solid basis for our beliefs. Bunyan's teachings show that he learned much from other preachers and writers in the Reformed tradition. However, his supreme and decisive authority was Holy Scripture, apart from which he would not speak. He appealed to his readers, "Give me the hearing, take me to the

10. Bunyan, *A Treatise of the Fear of God*, 28; see *Works*, 1:443.

11. Bunyan, *A Confession of My Faith*, 44–45; see *Works*, 2:601.

12. John Bunyan, *Relation of the Imprisonment of Mr. John Bunyan* (London: James Buckland, 1765), 36; see *Works*, 1:59.

13. John Bunyan, *A Discourse upon the Pharisee and the Publicane* (London: Joh. Harris, 1685), 94; see *Works*, 2:245.

14. John Bunyan, *The Holy City: or the New Jerusalem* (London: J. Dover, 1665), 91–92; see *Works*, 3:417.

15. John Bunyan, *Christ a Compleat Saviour: Or the Intercession of Christ, and Who Are Privileged in It*, in *Works* (1692), 391; see *Works*, 1:228.

Bible, and let me find in your heart no favor, if you find me to swerve from the Standard. . . . I have not written at a venture [randomly, or without good cause], nor borrowed my doctrine from libraries. I depend upon the sayings of no man. I found it in the Scriptures of truth, among the true sayings of God."[16]

A person's attitude toward the Bible says much about his attitude toward God. To believe God's Word is an act of worship toward God (see Acts 24:14).[17] Bunyan counseled, "Keep always close to your conscience the authority of the Word; fear the commandment as the commandment of a God both mighty and glorious, and as the commandment of a father both loving and pitiful [full of compassion]."[18]

Bunyan believed in reading the Bible frequently. Early on, he would have encountered Bayly's advice in *The Practice of Piety* on "how to read the Scriptures, once every year over, with ease, profit, and reverence."[19] W. R. Owens writes that Bunyan called for not just the "mere reading" of the Bible but for "a quite extraordinary immersion and absorption" in the text of Holy Scripture.[20] Bunyan modeled the results of such habits in his writings, which are an almost constant stream of biblical quotations and allusions. His quotations come mostly from the Authorized Version (the King James Version of 1611), but he showed a knowledge of the Geneva Bible (1560)[21] and even referred to the translation of William Tyndale (d. 1536).[22] Charles Spurgeon said that Bunyan is a great

16. John Bunyan, preface to *Light for Them that Sit in Darkness: Or, A Discourse of Jesus Christ* (London: Francis Smith, 1675), A3v–A4r; see *Works*, 1:392.

17. John Bunyan, *Instruction for the Ignorant* (London: Francis Smith, 1675), 34; see *Works*, 2:683

18. Bunyan, *A Treatise of the Fear of God*, 206; see *Works*, 1:485.

19. Cited in W. R. Owens, "John Bunyan and the Bible," in *The Cambridge Companion to Bunyan*, ed. Anne Dunan-Page (Cambridge, UK: Cambridge University Press, 2010), 42.

20. Owens, "John Bunyan and the Bible," 49.

21. Bunyan, *Works*, 1:395, 494, 513, 694; 2:88, 152, 377, 438; 3:406, 485, 710.

22. John Bunyan, *The Acceptable Sacrifice: Or the Excellency of a Broken Heart* (London: George Larkin, 1689), 45; see *Works*, 1:695.

example of a person who has eaten up the Scripture and taken it into his innermost being, writing, "Read anything of his, and you will see that it is almost like reading the Bible itself. . . . He has read it till his very soul was saturated with Scripture. . . . Prick him anywhere; his blood is bibline, the very essence of the Bible flows from him."[23]

Read the Bible with great expectation. Bunyan, quoting 2 Timothy 3:16, said, "Mark these words, 'All Scripture is profitable.' Mark, 'all,' take it where you will, and in what place you will."[24] For example, Bunyan said that, even though the ceremonies of the old covenant have passed away, they are still "a great help" to believers in revealing the work of Christ as the great priest and sacrifice. Therefore, he said, "I advise that you read the five books of Moses often."[25] Bunyan's stories abound with images of the written Word of God. The Bible is "the study" in the Palace Beautiful of God's church, where there are preserved "records of the greatest antiquity" about the Son of God and His people, written for "the comfort and solace of pilgrims."[26] The Bible is the sword of Valiant-for-truth; he wields "a right Jerusalem blade," a powerful weapon against the temptations of wicked men and fallen angels, and "its edges will never blunt."[27] It is the "map" to the Celestial City so that pilgrims will not lose their way.[28]

The Bible gives believers a spiritual vision of heavenly truth. The Word of God is the supernatural mirror that shows us ourselves in our sin and need and shows us the Lord in all His works and glory:

> It would present a man, one way, with his own feature exactly, and turn it but another way, and it would show one the very face

23. C. H. Spurgeon, "The Last Words of Christ on the Cross," sermon 2644, in *The Metropolitan Tabernacle Pulpit* (1899; repr., Pasadena, TX: Pilgrim Publications, 1977), 45:495.

24. Bunyan, *A Few Sighs from Hell*, 140; see *Works*, 3:708.

25. Bunyan, *Christ a Compleat Saviour*, in *Works* (1692), 400; see *Works*, 1:238.

26. Bunyan, *The Pilgrim's Progress*, 83–84; see *Works*, 3:110.

27. John Bunyan, *The Pilgrim's Progress, From This World to That Which Is to Come: The Second Part* (London: Nathaniel Ponder, 1684), 192; see *Works*, 3:233.

28. Bunyan, *The Pilgrim's Progress . . . The Second Part*, 202; see *Works*, 3:236.

> and similitude [likeness] of the Prince of pilgrims himself. Yea I have talked with them that can tell, and they have said that they have seen the very crown of thorns upon his head, by looking in that glass [mirror], they have therein also seen the holes in his hands, in his feet, and his side. Yea such an excellency is there in that glass, that it will show him to one where they have a mind to see him; whether living or dead, whether in earth or heaven, whether in a state of humiliation, or his exaltation, whether coming to suffer, or coming to reign.[29]

It is the sight of divine beauty in this mirror that moves the believing soul to receive all the Bible's teachings as good and precious. Bunyan said, "For the Scriptures carry such a blessed beauty in them to that soul that has faith in the things contained in them, that they do take the heart and captivate the soul of him that believes them, into the love and liking of them."[30]

Bunyan believed in the necessity of Scripture to live a godly life. Only on the authority of God's Word can we know what God considers to be a good work. Bunyan said, "Zeal without knowledge is like a mettled [high-spirited] horse without eyes, like a sword in a madman's hand." Without the Word, we have no wisdom (see Isa. 8:20).[31] It is the Devil's work to give men a low view of the Scriptures and to encourage them to depend on what is in their own minds and hearts.[32] Neither can people determine what is right based only on circumstances and opportunities that providence presents them. The only safe road is to follow the Word of God.[33] Bunyan

29. Bunyan, *The Pilgrim's Progress . . . The Second Part*, 187–88; see *Works*, 3:231.

30. Bunyan, *A Few Sighs from Hell*, 203; see *Works*, 3:720.

31. John Bunyan, *Christian Behaviour; Being the Fruits of True Christianity*, 3rd ed. (London: F. Smith, [1690]), 30; see *Works*, 2:554.

32. John Bunyan, "The Author to the Reader," in *Some Gospel-Truths Opened* (London: J. Wright, 1656), C7v; *A Few Sighs from Hell*, 151; see *Works*, 2:136; 3:710.

33. John Bunyan, *Exposition on the Ten First Chapters of Genesis, and Part of the Eleventh*, in *Works* (1692), 59; see *Works*, 2:482.

did more than just add some biblical ideas to his belief system; he planted himself in what one scholar called "the scripturally defined world," where the Bible became the basic interpreter of life and all things, shaping language itself.[34]

Bunyan affirmed the sufficiency of the Scriptures to guide mankind in spiritual things. Regarding one's salvation, he said, "Christian, you are not in this thing to follow your sense and feeling: but the very Word of God. . . . You must give more credit to one syllable of the written Word of the gospel, than you must give to all the saints and angels in heaven and earth."[35] Thus David Calhoun said that Bunyan held to "the regulative principle" that "in worship and doctrine we cannot go beyond what is written in the Bible."[36] The Word is "the rule of worship," and to substitute human traditions to direct our worship is a great backsliding from God.[37]

No human wisdom can supplant God's Word. He said, "The Holy Scriptures, of themselves, without the addition of human inventions, are able" to fully equip God's servants, to make the lost "wise unto salvation through faith in Jesus Christ," and to teach people how to worship God and walk righteously toward men (see 2 Tim. 3:15, 17).[38] He wrote, "The Scriptures spoken by the holy men of God are a sufficient rule to instruct to salvation them that do assuredly believe and close in with what they hold forth." Christ taught that men do not need a miraculous visitor from heaven: "They have Moses and the prophets; let them hear them" (Luke 16:29). Whether a person is ignorant, or breaking God's

34. John R. Knott Jr., "'Thou must live upon my Word': Bunyan and the Bible," in *John Bunyan: Conventicle and Parnassus; Tercentenary Essays*, ed. N. H. Keeble (Oxford: Clarendon Press, 1988), 159.

35. John Bunyan, *The Doctrine of the Law and Grace Unfolded* (London: M. Wright, 1659), 328; see *Works*, 1:562.

36. David B. Calhoun, *Grace Abounding: The Life, Books, and Influence of John Bunyan* (Ross-shire, UK: Christian Focus Publications, 2005), 170.

37. John Bunyan, *The Jerusalem Sinner Saved: Or, Good News for the Vilest of Men* (London: George Larkin, 1689), 4; see *Works*, 1:69.

38. Bunyan, *A Confession of My Faith*, 43; see *Works*, 2:601.

law, or in need of correction, or wavering, "that poor soul may not only be helped, but thoroughly furnished, not only to some, but to all good works."[39]

People should therefore "search the Scriptures," for "they are able to give a man perfect instruction into any of the things of God necessary to faith and godliness," if he has a heart to receive them.[40] However, Bunyan warned, do not study the Bible without making "a real application" of Christ to your soul, for the Scriptures testify of Jesus Christ (see John 5:39).[41]

Bunyan believed that a lack of reverence for the Word of God is the cause of "all disorders" of heart, life, conduct, and church. All sin begins with "wandering from the Word of God." He quoted Proverbs 13:13: "Whoso despiseth the word shall be destroyed: but he that feareth the commandment shall be rewarded." The Word is our life and safety (see Ps. 17:4; Prov. 4:20–22). In every age, the wicked reject the Word and follow their lusts and pride, but they will perish and be counted as fools (see Jer. 8:9; 44:16).[42] They do not believe that the Bible is the Word of God, in part because they do not see themselves as such bad sinners that they by nature deserve God's wrath and vengeance as the Bible says, and in part because worldly religious teachers tickle their ears with empty philosophy and deception (see Col. 2:8). By their rejection of God's Word, they provoke Him to anger (see Zech. 7:11–12).[43]

This is no call for nominal adherence to the Bible as God's Word. Bunyan warned that many people have "a notional and historical assent in the head" to the Bible, but their lives "deny, reject, and slight the Holy Scriptures."[44] When the Scriptures come with divine power, they kill sinners by the law (see 2 Cor. 3:6; Rom 7:9) and raise them

39. Bunyan, *A Few Sighs from Hell*, 140–41; see *Works*, 3:708.
40. Bunyan, *A Few Sighs from Hell*, 141; see *Works*, 3:708.
41. Bunyan, *A Few Sighs from Hell*, 148; see *Works*, 3:709.
42. Bunyan, *A Treatise of the Fear of God*, 29–31; see *Works*, 1:444.
43. Bunyan, *A Few Sighs from Hell*, 177–79, 183; see *Works*, 3:715–16.
44. Bunyan, *A Few Sighs from Hell*, 194; see *Works*, 3:718.

to a new life and comfort by the gospel (see John 6:63).[45] The truths of Christ become "precious and excellent" to them (1 Peter 1:8), and they stand in awe and greatly revere the Scriptures as God's Word.[46]

If we really believe that the Bible is God's Word, then we must be willing to obey it and proclaim it when men oppose it. Bunyan wrote, "This rebukes them that esteem the words and things of men more than the words of God, as those who are drawn from their respect of, and obedience to the Word of God by the pleasures or threats of men." Acknowledging the divine authority of the Bible is not enough; one must be willing to stand against the world in following it. Otherwise, the dread words of Christ will apply: "Whosoever therefore shall be ashamed of me and of my words in this adulterous and sinful generation; of him also shall the Son of man be ashamed, when he cometh in the glory of his Father with the holy angels" (Mark 8:38).[47]

The Word is fearful because its subject matter is the eternal destiny of sinners. Scripture reveals "eternal glory" and "eternal fire," and how we respond to the Bible determines which one represents our future (see John 12:48). Therefore, we should tremble at the Word, for it alone guides us in how to please God.[48] God would rather send thousands of souls to hell than violate His holy Word, so do not rest until your soul is converted to Jesus Christ as the Word commands.[49] On the other hand, God's Word is completely trustworthy and divinely powerful to save sinners. It is the Word of Christ. When Prince Emmanuel approaches the rebellious town of Mansoul, He declares, "All my words are true, I am mighty to save."[50] This is the hope of sinners and the confidence of preachers.

45. Bunyan, *A Few Sighs from Hell*, 195–200; see *Works*, 3:718.
46. Bunyan, *A Few Sighs from Hell*, 201–2; see *Works*, 3:720.
47. Bunyan, *A Treatise of the Fear of God*, 31–32; see *Works*, 1:444.
48. Bunyan, *A Treatise of the Fear of God*, 27–28; see *Works*, 1:443.
49. Bunyan, *A Few Sighs from Hell*, 153; see *Works*, 3:710.
50. John Bunyan, *The Holy War, Made by Shaddai upon Diabolus . . . Or, the Losing and Taking Again of the Town of Mansoul* (London: Nat. Ponder, 1696), 101; see *Works*, 3:289.

Do you receive the Bible as the Word of God? To do so involves a belief in its truthfulness, and also a heart-attitude of trust and fear. When you read the Bible, you must do so knowing that this is the voice of the Lord. When you hear the preaching of the Word, you must know that the Judge and Savior is speaking to you. And if you are a preacher, then you must preach as a herald of the holy King.

Preaching the Word with Fear and Trembling

Bunyan's holy fear of God overflowed into his view of the ministry of the Word. We can see this in his stories of *The Pilgrim's Progress.* Shortly after Christian passed through the gate into the narrow way of salvation, he came to the house of Interpreter. This wise teacher (a symbol of the Holy Spirit)[51] brought the pilgrim to a room where he saw the picture of a very serious person on the wall. Bunyan described the picture: "It had eyes lifted up to heaven, the best of books in his hand, the law of truth was written upon its lips, the world was behind his back; it stood as if it pleaded with men, and a crown of gold did hang over its head."[52] This remarkable person is further described as a spiritual father, the ideal pattern of a good pastor who "is the only man, whom the Lord of the place whither you are going, has authorized to be your guide."[53] Later, when Christiana and the children followed her husband, Interpreter sent with them his servant "Great-heart" with sword, helmet, and shield to guide and defend them.[54] Great-heart taught them of the person and work of Jesus Christ, fought against a giant that assaulted

51. Interpreter's actions show him as signifying the Holy Spirit. He has someone light a candle for Christian, which the marginal note identifies as "illumination" (*The Pilgrim's Progress*, 37; see *Works*, 3:98). His house is like the Bible, full of images of spiritual truth. In the second part of *The Pilgrim's Progress*, Interpreter arranges for the pilgrims to have a bath (margin: "the bath of sanctification") and seals each of them with his mark. Their pastor, Great-heart, is a servant of Interpreter, calls him "my Lord," and comes and goes at his command (*The Pilgrim's Progress . . . The Second Part*, 51–53, 71, 92; see *Works*, 3:189, 190, 197, 204).

52. Bunyan, *The Pilgrim's Progress*, 37–38; see *Works*, 3:98.

53. Bunyan, *The Pilgrim's Progress*, 38–39; see *Works*, 3:98.

54. Bunyan, *The Pilgrim's Progress . . . The Second Part*, 53; see *Works*, 3:190.

them in the way, and led them past frightening lions.[55] However, he was a man under authority ("at my Lord's command") and performed his service only as it was granted him.[56]

Bunyan had a high view of the pastoral ministry. As the images just cited reveal, he saw the pastor as a heavenly minded guide who has renounced this world, a brave soldier for the Lord who defends God's people, a teacher of the gospel of Christ, an ardent preacher to sinners. Bunyan learned this view of pastoral ministry from the Scriptures and from his personal experiences with men such as John Gifford and John Burton. Yet he did not exalt ministers too highly. The preacher is only a servant of God and a conduit of God's truth. He is like a "cloud" that draws its water "out of the sea" and pours rain down on the earth: "ministers should fetch their doctrine from God" and "should give out what they know of God to the world."[57]

Bunyan did not thrust himself into the ministry, but he was called by the church. Five or six years after he was awakened to his sins and enabled to trust in Jesus Christ, though he was still oscillating between fear and assurance, some of the more mature saints in his church recognized his ability to express biblical truth to the edification of others. They urged him "to speak a word of exhortation" at one of the church meetings. Bunyan felt afraid and weak, but he did speak at two private gatherings and received good feedback. They took him along on evangelistic trips into the countryside, and again his private admonitions proved to build up his listeners. Consequently, the church appointed Bunyan "to a more ordinary and public preaching the Word" after a time of prayer and fasting.[58]

Bunyan felt himself "most unworthy" and preached "with great fear and trembling at the sight of my own weakness." On the other

55. Bunyan, *The Pilgrim's Progress . . . The Second Part*, 54–58, 68–69; see *Works*, 3:190–91, 195–96.

56. Bunyan, *The Pilgrim's Progress . . . The Second Part*, 71; see *Works*, 3:197.

57. Bunyan, *The Pilgrim's Progress . . . The Second Part*, 87; see *Works*, 3:203.

58. John Bunyan, *Grace Abounding to the Chief of Sinners*, 8th ed. (London: Nath. Ponder, 1692), 136–38; see *Works*, 1:40–41.

hand, he was encouraged by biblical statements such as "They have addicted themselves to the ministry of the saints" (1 Cor. 16:15) and by the examples of godly people reported in Foxe's *Acts and Monuments* (also known as Foxe's *Book of Martyrs*). He described his preaching as a mixture of compassion to lost sinners and warnings that awakened and afflicted them over their sins and need of Jesus Christ.[59] His preaching was strengthened by his own heart experience of the fear of God. He said, "I preached what I felt, what I smartingly [painfully] did feel, even that under which my poor soul did groan and tremble to astonishment." He was not a fire-and-brimstone preacher who looked down on unbelievers, but was one who lived with a "fire in mine own conscience."[60]

After Bunyan had preached in this way for two years, the Lord brought him to a more settled "peace and comfort through Christ." Accordingly, his preaching changed. While still preaching so as to undermine self-righteousness, he dwelt more upon Jesus Christ in His offices and graces. Later, God taught him more about the doctrine of union with Christ. These three points—sin, Christ, and union with Christ—became the major themes of his preaching until he was imprisoned. He was never a theoretical preacher but was one who combined biblical doctrine with biblical experience. Through it all, Bunyan said, "I preached what I saw and felt."[61] Bunyan exemplified preaching with a hearty sense of the reality of divine things—the sense that faith and the fear of the Lord bring to the soul.

The faithful preacher must both warn and comfort men through the truth of divine realities. In *The Pilgrim's Progress*, Christian and Hopeful come to the Delectable Mountains, where they meet some kind shepherds who cared for the sheep for whom Prince Emmanuel died. Bunyan identified these shepherds as the teachers of God's truth, writing, "Thus by the shepherds, secrets are revealed,

59. Bunyan, *Grace Abounding*, 139–40; see *Works*, 1:41.
60. Bunyan, *Grace Abounding*, 142; see *Works*, 1:41.
61. Bunyan, *Grace Abounding*, 143; see *Works*, 1:41.

which from all other men are kept concealed." Their names reveal their character and calling: "Knowledge, Experience, Watchful, and Sincere." On the one hand, they took the pilgrims to see Hill Error, with its steep cliff from which men fall to their death. From Mount Caution they saw men blinded by Giant Despair after they had wandered from the way. Even that far into the journey to the Celestial City, they saw a doorway into hell, where some professing Christians such as Judas and Ananias had fallen away. These things made them tremble with fear. On the other hand, the shepherds let them look through a "perspective glass," or telescope, to see something of the glory of heaven.[62] Bunyan believed that a pastor's calling was to help pilgrims see the spiritual realities that, though invisible to the eye, have eternal weight and significance.

Bunyan preached with a heartfelt desire for his hearers to experience the power of the Word unto salvation. He "with great earnestness cried to God" for the conversion of people. "O that they who have heard me speak this day, did but see as I do, what sin, death, hell, and the curse of God is; and also what the grace, and love, and mercy of God is through Christ." Bunyan was opposed and criticized, especially by the more educated clergy of the established church.[63] He was also accused of being a Jesuit, a witch, a robber, and a fornicator, and of having two wives at once. Nevertheless, he gloried in these slanders, because false accusations are a sign of being a true saint and child of God (see Matt. 5:11).[64] Bunyan felt God's empowerment in preaching as if an angel stood behind him to encourage him. He preached the gospel of Christ with "power and heavenly evidence upon my own soul, while I have been laboring to unfold it, to demonstrate it, and to fasten it upon the conscience of others."[65] His heart for the lost drove him "into the darkest places

62. Bunyan, *The Pilgrim's Progress*, 207–13; see *Works*, 3:143–45.
63. Bunyan, *Grace Abounding*, 144–45; see *Works*, 1:42.
64. Bunyan, *Grace Abounding*, 156; see *Works*, 1:45.
65. Bunyan, *Grace Abounding*, 144–45; see *Works*, 1:42.

of the country," where few people professed to have faith in Christ, for he longed for conversions as for children.[66]

The preacher faces many temptations, even in the act of preaching. Bunyan reported being assaulted with blasphemous thoughts during his sermon so that he had to restrain himself from blurting them out. Sometimes he started to preach, but then felt so spiritually hindered that it was "as if my head had been in a bag." Satan tempted him to avoid preaching on Scriptures that confronted his own sins, but Bunyan chose to let the Word judge him even as he preached it to others.[67]

When preaching, Bunyan was "often tempted to pride and liftings up of heart." The Lord mercifully countered such temptations in a number of ways. Bunyan wrote that God daily showed him something of "the evil of my own heart" and the "multitude of corruptions and infirmities" in it. God also used the Scriptures to remind him that gifts and abilities are nothing without love (see 1 Cor. 13:1–2). Bunyan learned to see his preaching as a "fiddle" that Christ played to make music for the church. Shall a mere fiddle be proud? He also remembered that spiritual gifts will pass away, but love will last forever (see 1 Cor. 13:8). People may be able to preach well but in the end still go to hell. People with little gifts in knowledge or speech may have a thousand times more grace than those who can preach like angels, and so be much the more pleasing to God. Bunyan concluded, "A little grace, a little love, a little of the true fear of God is better than all these gifts."[68]

Bunyan also learned to regard his preaching in the light of the needs of the church and the approaching judgment day. It helps the preacher to "be little in his own eyes" when he remembers "that his gifts are not his own, but the church's, and that by them he is made a servant of the church, and he must also give at last an

66. Bunyan, *Grace Abounding*, 148–49; see *Works*, 1:43.
67. Bunyan, *Grace Abounding*, 150–51; see *Works*, 1:44.
68. Bunyan, *Grace Abounding*, 151–53; see *Works*, 1:44–45.

account of his stewardship unto the Lord Jesus, and to give a good account will be a blessed thing." Therefore, Bunyan wrote, "Let all men therefore prize a little with the fear of the Lord; gifts indeed are desirable, but yet great grace and small gifts are better than great gifts and no grace." Only grace leads to glory.[69]

There is a majesty about the ministry of the Word, but let us never forget that it is the majesty not of the minister but of the Master whom he serves. Pray for the pastors of the church and teachers of the Bible, that they would exercise their ministry in holy fear as stewards whom the Lord will hold accountable. Pray that they would be careful not just to preach the Word well but also to live the Word well. And, if you are a preacher, then pray for yourself—and tremble.

69. Bunyan, *Grace Abounding*, 154–55; see *Works*, 1:45.

8

Persevering by the Power of Godly Fear

Bunyan was a man of perseverance. As we have seen, he would rather let moss grow on his eyebrows in prison than compromise his calling to preach the Word of God.[1] He suffered twelve years of unjust incarceration and later returned to prison again. Yet when his mouth was silenced, his pen was busy, and his witness to Christ blazes in his books. Sinful men could bind his body but not his soul. Out of his sufferings have flowed blessings for many.

Bunyan's troubles brought depth and maturity to his teachings. George Whitefield said that *The Pilgrim's Progress* "smells of the prison." It is saturated by godliness proven in the furnaces of fiery trials. Whitefield explained, in his preface to the 1767 *Works* of Bunyan,

> Ministers never write or preach so well as when under the cross. The Spirit of Christ and of glory then rests upon them. It was this,

1. John Bunyan, "To the Reader," in *A Confession of My Faith, and A Reason of My Practice* (London: Francis Smith, 1672), A6v; see *Works*, 2:594.

> no doubt, that made the Puritans of the last century such burning and shining lights. When cast out by the Black Bartholomew Act [Act of Uniformity of 1662], and driven from their respective charges to preach in barns and fields, in the highways and hedges, they in an especial manner wrote and preached as men having authority. Though dead, by their writings they yet speak. A peculiar unction attends them to this very hour.[2]

Whether we are ministers, or Christians of various callings, or non-Christians counting the cost of whether to follow Jesus, we can learn much from Bunyan about perseverance in the fear of the Lord. To encourage Christians to persevere, Bunyan presented God's precious and comforting promises to those who fear Him, and he also taught that God's grace preserves His people in the fear of the Lord so that they can and will make it to the end.

God's Promises of Blessing to Those Who Fear Him

Bunyan said, "It seems to me, as if this grace of fear is the darling grace, the grace that God sets his heart upon at the highest rate. As it were he embraces and hugs and lays the man in his bosom that hath and grows strong in this grace of the fear of God."[3] The Lord expresses His delight in this grace through His many promises given to those who possess it. Knowing these promises encourages believers to persevere in the fear of the Lord and to grow in it.

God gives the person who fears the Lord "a grant and a license to trust" that the Lord is his God and his salvation. Psalm 115:11 says, "Ye that fear the LORD, trust in the LORD: he is their help and their shield." Bunyan marvels in this promise, for it goes beyond

2. George Whitefield, preface to *The Works of that Eminent Servant of Christ Mr. John Bunyan,* 3rd ed. (London: W. Johnston, 1767), 1:iii.

3. John Bunyan, *A Treatise of the Fear of God* (London: N. Ponder, 1679), 183; see *Works,* 1:479.

the general exhortation to all people that they should trust in the Lord, but singles out those who fear the Lord and offers them this assurance: "He is their help and their shield. Their help under all their weaknesses and infirmities, and a shield to defend them against all the assaults of the devil, and this world."[4]

God promises to be not only the Savior of those who fear Him but also their "teacher and guide." Psalm 25:12 says, "What man is he that feareth the LORD? him shall he teach in the way that he shall choose." Though the Christian may be ignorant about many things and faces many who tempt him to turn aside, God promises to lead him to glory. The Lord will walk with him, and communion with God will make the journey "sweet and pleasant," Bunyan said.[5] God will teach him the secret things of Jesus Christ, "all the treasures of wisdom and knowledge" (Col. 2:3), revealed in Christ's person, offices, and relationship to His people and in His covenant (see Ps. 25:14). Such truth will ravish the believer's heart.[6]

Bunyan also quoted the promise of Psalm 33:18–19:

> Behold, the eye of the LORD is upon them that fear him, upon
> them that hope in his mercy;
> to deliver their soul from death, and to keep them alive in famine.

God watches over them, not to accuse and destroy them for their sins, but to delight in them and deliver them from death, especially from spiritual and eternal death.[7] God sends the armies of heaven to camp around those who fear him—angels in invisible chariots of fire (see 2 Kings 6:17; Ps. 34:7; Heb. 1:14). The angels have the power to blind, terrify, and kill the enemies of God's people—even the most powerful monarch cannot resist them (see Gen. 19:10–11;

4. Bunyan, *A Treatise of the Fear of God*, 134–35; see *Works*, 1:468.
5. Bunyan, *A Treatise of the Fear of God*, 135–37; see *Works*, 1:468.
6. Bunyan, *A Treatise of the Fear of God*, 137–38; see *Works*, 1:468.
7. Bunyan, *A Treatise of the Fear of God*, 139; see *Works*, 1:469.

2 Kings 7:6; Acts 12:21–23).[8] God's own salvation is near to them, to rescue them from all the powers of the Devil, sin, and death (see Ps. 85:9).[9]

God also promises His provision: those who fear the Lord will not lack any good thing (see Ps. 34:9–10). Well aware of the sufferings that believers experience, Bunyan nevertheless saw this as a precious promise of kind providence to order all events. He said, "Not anything that God sees good for them, shall those men want [lack] that fear the Lord. If *health* will do them good, if *sickness* will do them good, if *riches* will do them good, if *poverty* will do them good, if *life* will do them good, if *death* will do them good, then they shall not want [lack] them."[10]

Someone might say that this is not the good that such people desire, but Bunyan has another promise for them. Psalm 145:19 says, "He will fulfil the desire of them that fear him: he also will hear their cry, and will save them." Here is a royal promise indeed. God promises to give them all that they desire (see Ps. 20:4–5). All the desires of those who fear the Lord will ultimately be fulfilled in God's glorious presence. Though it may be a long time in coming, Bunyan says, "Learn first to live upon your portion in the promise of it, and that will make your expectation of it sweet."[11] God promises, "Delight thyself also in the LORD; and he shall give thee the desires of thine heart" (Ps. 37:4). Christians should not fear that God's goodness will be too small for their desires. The opposite is true. Bunyan said, "He goes beyond their desires, beyond their apprehensions, beyond what their hearts could conceive to ask for. . . . They desire a *handful*, God gives them a *sea-full*."[12]

8. Bunyan, *A Treatise of the Fear of God*, 141–43; see *Works*, 1:469–70.
9. Bunyan, *A Treatise of the Fear of God*, 143–44; see *Works*, 1:470.
10. Bunyan, *A Treatise of the Fear of God*, 140; see *Works*, 1:469.
11. Bunyan, *A Treatise of the Fear of God*, 150–51; see *Works*, 1:471.
12. Bunyan, *The Desire of the Righteous Granted*, in *Works* (1692), 245–46; see *Works*, 1:761.

The greatest good that God promises to give to those who fear Him is His love: "But the mercy of the LORD is from everlasting to everlasting upon them that fear him" (Ps. 103:17). The words "from everlasting to everlasting," Bunyan said, declare "the eternity of God himself." Therefore the promise is that, as long as God has His being, those who fear Him will receive mercy. Bunyan assured the child of God, "This is long-lived mercy. It will live longer than your sin, it will live longer than temptation, it will live longer than your sorrows, it will live longer than your persecutors." God's love is an infinite promise, one that Bunyan urged his readers to "hang . . . like a chain of gold about your neck." "For as the heaven is high above the earth, so great is his mercy toward them that fear him" (Ps. 103:11).[13]

God engages the infinite affections of His heart toward His children and sympathizes tenderly with them in their afflictions and temptations (see Judg. 10:16; Ps. 103:13; Isa. 63:9; Heb. 2:17–18; 4:15). He is a Father to them, and He can never forget His dear children or fail to be compassionate toward them (see Isa. 49:15; James 5:11).[14] The Lord takes pleasure in those who fear Him (see Ps. 147:11). God delights in His Son, in His works, and in those who fear Him. His delights will be the river of joy from which they drink in His presence (see Ps. 36:8). His pleasure in them expresses itself in the way that He makes them beautiful (see Ps. 149:4). He teaches them how to please Him in all their ways (see Prov. 11:20; 1 Thess. 4:1) and is "ravished" with them (Song 4:9). He bears patiently with their faults (see Mal. 3:16–17) and takes great delight in the smallest acts of obedience and worship that they give Him (see Mark 12:41–44).[15] He is a tenderhearted Father.

Bunyan encouraged believers to sing the promises of God in order to comfort themselves and each other. He offered to them

13. Bunyan, *A Treatise of the Fear of God*, 144–46; see *Works*, 1:470.

14. Bunyan, *A Treatise of the Fear of God*, 147–48; see *Works*, 1:470–71.

15. Bunyan, *A Treatise of the Fear of God*, 151, 152, 153 [irregular pagination, sig. L3v–L4v]; see *Works*, 1:471–72.

the metrical version of Psalm 128 from the Sternhold and Hopkins Psalter, which begins,

> Blessed art thou that fearest God,
> And walkest in his way
> For of thy labor thou shalt eat
> Happy art thou, I say.[16]

Bunyan's teaching on the fear of God defies all preconceived notions. He offers a biblical blend of fear, love, hope, and joy that diminishes none of these qualities but enhances and intensifies each. Here is the radiantly joyful fear and the humble, trembling hope that Christ gives His people in the presence of the living God. It is an astonishing combination—the only one that can satisfy the souls of mankind. Drink deeply from this well, and you will find life and the strength to persevere through many sorrows.

God's Promises of Perseverance to Those Who Fear Him

In addition to encouraging those who fear the Lord with God's promises, Bunyan also taught the necessity and grace of perseverance.[17] Bunyan's emphasis on God's grace did not reduce the importance of pressing on in faithfulness but empowered it. As illustrated in *The Pilgrim's Progress*, the Christian life is a constant struggle to persevere on the way to heaven. Perseverance is necessary to enter glory. Bunyan said,

> To be saved is to be preserved in the faith to the end. "He that shall endure unto the end, the same shall be saved" (Matt. 24:13).

16. Bunyan, *A Treatise of the Fear of God*, 156; see *Works*, 1:473. On the psalm, see Thomas Sternhold, John Hopkins, et al., *The Whole Booke of Psalmes: Collected into English Meeter* (London: by G. M. for the Company of Stationers, 1644), 85.

17. Portions of this section are adapted from Joel R. Beeke, "Bunyan's Perseverance," in *The Pure Flame of Devotion: The History of Christian Spirituality*, ed. G. Stephen Weaver Jr. and Ian Hugh Clary (Kitchener, Ontario: Joshua Press, 2013), 323–41.

> Not that perseverance is an accident in Christianity, or a thing performed by human industry. They that are saved "are kept by the power of God, through faith unto salvation" (1 Peter 1:3–5). But perseverance is absolutely necessary to the complete saving of the soul. . . . He that goes to sea with a purpose to arrive at Spain, cannot arrive there if he be drowned by the way. Wherefore perseverance is absolutely necessary to the saving of the soul.[18]

As surely as perseverance is necessary, so surely is perseverance given by God to His people through Jesus Christ. Robert Richey writes, "The Puritans and Bunyan were kinsmen in their belief in the doctrine of the saints' final and complete perseverance."[19] Bunyan believed in salvation by grace from beginning to end. God the Father graciously provides in Christ a sufficient treasury of all spiritual blessings for His chosen ones (see Eph. 1:3–4; 2 Tim. 1:9). From this treasury, He shares with them what they need so that He preserves them in the faith and they faithfully persevere through life.[20]

This is not to say that every professing Christian will persevere to the end. Bunyan understood well that a person can be very religious and yet not be saved, and so not continue in outward acts of morality and religion to the end. Bunyan himself at one period of his life had an active conscience, cleaned up his conduct, went to church, and read the Puritans—but was still perishing without saving faith in Christ. He warned that men have many ways to get rid of conviction of sin, including busyness in religion.[21] Apart from God's gift of life, we have no true godliness in which to persevere. Bunyan wrote, "Wherefore sinners, before faith, are compared to

18. Bunyan, *Saved by Grace*, in *Works* (1692), 556; see *Works*, 1:339.

19. Robert A. Richey, "The Puritan Doctrine of Sanctification: Constructions of the Saints' Final Perseverance and Complete Perseverance as Mirrored in Bunyan's 'The Pilgrim's Progress'" (ThD Dissertation, Mid-America Baptist Theological Seminary, Schenectady, NY, 1990), 220.

20. Bunyan, *Saved by Grace*, in *Works* (1692), 560; see *Works*, 1:344.

21. Bunyan, *Saved by Grace*, in *Works* (1692), 567; see *Works*, 1:351.

the wilderness, whose fruits are briars and thorns . . . they are said to be Godless, Christless, Spiritless, faithless, hopeless. . . . Now, these things being thus, it is impossible that all the men under heaven, that are unconverted, should be able to bring forth one work rightly good. . . . Good works must come from a good heart."[22]

However, when God gives a person to Christ, so that he comes to Christ in hungry faith, Christ will keep him safe to the end. Our Lord said in John 6:37–39,

> All that the Father giveth me shall come to me; and him that cometh to me I will in no wise cast out. For I came down from heaven, not to do mine own will, but the will of him that sent me. And this is the Father's will which hath sent me, that of all which he hath given me I should lose nothing, but should raise it up again at the last day.

This is the unbreakable chain forged in heaven: the Father gives in regeneration, the soul comes in faith, and Christ saves to the end. In Bunyan's treatise on John 6:37, he wrote, "Christ is as full in his resolution to save those given to him as is the Father in giving of them. Christ prizes the gift of his Father; he will lose nothing of it."[23] Both Father and Son will keep their covenant.

Greaves writes that, for Bunyan, "preservation and perseverance were not possible apart from the intercessory work of Christ."[24] Hebrews 7:25–26 describes Christ's work of keeping the saints in terms of His intercession as their priest:

> Wherefore he is able also to save them to the uttermost that come unto God by him, seeing he ever liveth to make intercession for

22. John Bunyan, *Christian Behaviour; Being the Fruits of True Christianity,* 3rd ed. (London: F. Smith, [1690]), 13–14; see *Works,* 2:551.

23. John Bunyan, *Come, and Welcome, to Jesus Christ,* 4th ed. (London: by J. A. for John Harris, 1688), 41; see *Works,* 1:254.

24. Richard L. Greaves, *John Bunyan,* Courtenay Studies in Reformation Theology 2 (Grand Rapids: Eerdmans, 1969), 91.

> them. For such an high priest became us, who is holy, harmless, undefiled, separate from sinners, and made higher than the heavens.

Bunyan wrote that Christ's enduring intercession proves that God's covenant of grace to Christians "is not shaken, broken, or made invalid by all their weaknesses and infirmities."[25] Why not? It is not shaken because the covenant stands upon Christ's work, not ours. Bunyan said, "He is the Lord our righteousness, and he is the Savior of the body, so that my sins break not the covenant; but them notwithstanding, God's covenant stands fast with him, with him forevermore."[26]

Furthermore, the saints find in Jesus Christ such beauty and life that they will not let Him go for all the world. Bunyan turned for examples not just to the Bible, but also to the martyrs of the church recorded in Foxe's *Acts and Monuments*. Ignatius found something in Christ so precious that he chose to suffer the torments of the Devil rather than lose Christ. Romanus said to an enraged dictator, "Your sentence, O Emperor, I joyfully embrace, and refuse not to be sacrificed—by as cruel torments as you can invent." Menas said to his torturers that nothing compared to the kingdom of heaven and that he had learned not to fear those who kill the body, but Him who can destroy body and soul in hell. Eulalia rejoiced in the victory of Christ even as they tortured her. Agnus willingly received the sword into her chest so that she could escape this dark world and go to her heavenly husband, Jesus Christ. All these people did this, Bunyan said, because they found something in Jesus Christ that they could find nowhere else: in Him they found God, grace, life, glory, and righteousness.[27]

Bunyan's vision of perseverance has strengthened persecuted Christians throughout the world. When *The Pilgrim's Progress* was first translated into the language of the people of Madagascar, Africa,

25. Bunyan, *Christ a Compleat Saviour*, in *Works* (1692), 394; see *Works*, 1:231.
26. Bunyan, *Christ a Compleat Saviour*, in *Works* (1692), 395; see *Works*, 1:232.
27. Bunyan, *Come, and Welcome, to Jesus Christ*, 175–78; see *Works*, 1:295–96.

believers there were suffering intense persecution. They passed around eight handwritten copies of Bunyan's book, identifying deeply with Christian's battle with Apollyon and his sufferings in the Valley of the Shadow of Death. One believer wrote, "O God, do thou enable us to make the progress that Pilgrim made, and if thy kingdom in Madagascar is to be advanced by these means [that is, by their suffering persecution], be it so."[28]

Perseverance is not easy. Perseverance demands a willingness to suffer long for Christ. Christianity is a long-distance race. Its trials may not be the spectacular sorrows of the martyrs, but the daily grind of difficult obedience stretched over months and years can be just as hard. Paul wrote, "Know ye not that they which run in a race run all, but one receiveth the prize? So run, that ye may obtain" (1 Cor. 9:24). Bunyan said, "It is an easy matter for a man to run hard for a spurt, for a furlong [an eighth of a mile], for a mile or two. Oh, but to hold out for a hundred, for a thousand, for ten thousand miles! That man that does this, he must look to meet with cross, pain, and wearisomeness to the flesh, especially if, as he goes, he meets with briars and quagmires, and other encumbrances that make his journey so much the more painful."[29]

Believers do not ride to heaven in victory chariots but sometimes must trudge through life like Christiana's children walking through a misty swamp at night, with bushes entangling them and mud pulling their shoes off their feet.[30] The Christian can experience discouragement, depression, and spiritual darkness, as Bunyan did in seasons of his imprisonment. He wrote, "I was once above all the rest in a very sad and low condition for many weeks. . . . For indeed at that time

28. David B. Calhoun, *Grace Abounding: The Life, Books, and Influence of John Bunyan* (Ross-shire, UK: Christian Focus Publications, 2005), 61.

29. John Bunyan, *The Heavenly Foot-man: Or, A Description of the Man that Gets to Heaven* (London: Charles Doe, 1698), 33; see *Works*, 3:387. The original ends with the words "the more painfuller."

30. John Bunyan, *The Pilgrim's Progress, From This World to That Which Is to Come: The Second Part* (London: Nathaniel Ponder, 1684), 201; see *Works*, 3:236

all the things of God were hid from my soul."[31] On another occasion, when it was Bunyan's turn to preach to his fellow prisoners, he found himself to be "empty, spiritless, and barren," until finally, after prayerful meditation on the Word, God gave him a glimpse of the glory of heaven that refreshed his soul and enabled him to preach.[32]

How then does the Lord preserve His people so that they persevere? God meets with His people in their sorrows and temptations. Though the Devil pours water on their hearts to quench the fire of their godliness, Christ is always (though often in a way that believers cannot perceive) pouring in the oil of grace so that they will persevere and burn all the hotter for the Lord.[33] In prison, Bunyan experienced both darkness and light. Bunyan said of one season in prison, "I never had in all my life so great an inlet into the Word of God as now." He said that portions of the Bible that were closed to him before "are made in this place and state to shine upon me; Jesus Christ also was never more real and apparent than now; here I have seen him and felt him indeed."[34]

The spiritual sight of Christ keeps believers going when they enjoy a dazzling sense of divine glory or in those times when their sight is dim. Either way, they live by an inward sense of unseen realities. Bunyan said, "For when men do come to see the things of another world, what a God, what a Christ, what a heaven, and what an eternal glory there is to be enjoyed; also, when they see that it is possible for them to have a share in it, I tell you it will make them run through thick and thin to enjoy it."[35] As we have seen, Bunyan closely connects this spiritual sense with faith and godly fear.

31. John Bunyan, *Grace Abounding to the Chief of Sinners,* 8th ed. (London: Nath. Ponder, 1692), 169; see *Works,* 1:49.

32. John Bunyan, "The Epistle to the Readers," in *The Holy City: or the New Jerusalem* (London: J. Dover, 1665), A3r; see *Works,* 3:397. See chapter two of this book on Bunyan's imprisonments.

33. John Bunyan, *The Pilgrim's Progress from This World, to That Which Is to Come,* 3rd ed. (London: Nath. Ponder, 1679), 44–45; see *Works,* 3:100.

34. Bunyan, *Grace Abounding,* 162; see *Works,* 1:47.

35. Bunyan, *The Heavenly Foot-man,* 38; see *Works,* 3:388.

Not only a sense of the reality of heaven, but also a sense of the reality of the coming judgment, strengthened Bunyan to endure persecution without compromising his faith. Once, a representative of the Church of England urged Bunyan to promise to stop preaching so that he could be released from prison. Bunyan replied, "Sir, Wycliffe says that he which leaves off preaching and hearing of the Word of God for fear of excommunication of men, he is already excommunicated of God, and shall in the day of judgment be counted a traitor to Christ."[36]

A major influence by which God preserves His people is the fear of God. God has promised that when He places godly fear in the heart of a people, "they shall not depart from me" (Jer. 32:40). Their future is secure: "It shall be well with them that fear God" (Eccl. 8:12). God gives this grace both to join their hearts to Him and to keep them from finally falling away, though they pass through many "temptations, difficulties, snares, traps, trials, and troubles."[37] Proverbs 28:14 says, "Happy is the man that feareth alway." Bunyan said that such a man is "happy already" and "happy for the time to come," because this grace of fear will never end but will "continue till the soul that has it is brought unto the mansion house of glory."[38]

How does the fear of God guard the believer from sliding into damnation? Bunyan said that if a person is like a "town," then the heart is "the main fort." Godly fear is not just in the head (as knowledge) and not just in the mouth (as talk), but it guards the heart and therefore keeps a man safe. In particular, Bunyan said that, in the heart, the grace of fear principally works upon the faculty of the will. The will sets the fundamental direction of the soul, either to heaven or to hell, for it leads all the rest of the powers of the

36. John Bunyan, *Relation of the Imprisonment of Mr. John Bunyan* (London: James Buckland, 1765), 35; see *Works*, 1:59.

37. Bunyan, *A Treatise of the Fear of God*, 219; see *Works*, 1:488.

38. Bunyan, *A Treatise of the Fear of God*, 218; see *Works*, 1:488.

soul.[39] The fear of the Lord is the King's trusted and special friend, whom he sets over the main fort to keep it "in the subjection and obedience of the gospel." Indeed, it is among the graces the one "most tender of God's honor," and therefore it proves to be an alert watchman against the enemy.[40]

Bunyan illustrated this principle with the battle for the town of Mansoul in his allegory *The Holy War.* Sometime after the conversion of Mansoul back to Prince Emmanuel, the town began to backslide into spiritual complacency and laziness. A wicked man named Mr. Carnal-security (the son of Lady Fear-nothing) won over its inhabitants, so that they no longer sought their prince or depended upon him, and instead grieved the Lord High Secretary (signifying the Holy Spirit). But a bold person named Mr. Godly-fear rebuked Carnal-security and awakened the conscience of the people of the town. Under the leadership of Mr. Godly-fear, they put Carnal-security to death and sent repeated petitions to Prince Emmanuel for grace and forgiveness.[41] Thus, the fear of God plays a crucial role in awakening a Christian when he becomes spiritually sleepy and fails to walk zealously by faith in Christ alone.

Sensing that Mansoul was spiritually weak, its enemy Diabolus returned to besiege it again with temptations to sin. At one point, the evil armies penetrated its gates, forcing the soldiers of Shaddai to retreat into the castle. This "castle" represents the heart of man.[42] The episode signifies a Christian's succumbing to sin, but, despite this, the Devil being unable to regain his rule over the heart. The reason why he cannot reveals Bunyan's view of how God preserves His saints. Bunyan wrote, "Diabolus made a great many attempts to have broken open the gates of the castle, but Mr. Godly-fear was

39. Bunyan, *A Treatise of the Fear of God*, 220–21; see *Works*, 1:488.

40. Bunyan, *A Treatise of the Fear of God*, 222–23; see *Works*, 1:488.

41. John Bunyan, *The Holy War, Made by Shaddai upon Diabolus . . . Or, the Losing and Taking Again of the Town of Mansoul* (London: Nat. Ponder, 1696), 203–19; see *Works*, 3:324–29.

42. Bunyan, *The Holy War*, 3; see *Works*, 3:255.

made the keeper of that; and he was a man of that courage, conduct, and valor" so that, as long as he lived, Diabolus could never succeed, leading Bunyan to make the parenthetical comment, "I have wished sometimes that that man [Mr. Godly-fear] had had the whole rule of the town of Mansoul."[43] A Christian may be overrun by sin for a time, but godly fear will keep his heart clinging to the Lord, and, the more his fear grows, the more holy he will be.

Why is this godly fear so effective in keeping believers from totally and finally falling away from Christ? The answer lies in its source. After all the battles had been won, Prince Emmanuel told Mansoul, "The way of backsliding was yours, but the way and means of your recovery was mine. . . . It was I that set Mr. Godly-fear to work in Mansoul."[44]

Christians discouraged by their sins and the weakness of their faith may take heart in knowing that their Lord sustains godly fear in their hearts and so guards them. What a blessed gift this grace is, that makes Christians watchful and guards Christ's throne in their hearts. Let them love the fear of the Lord, fan it into flame by exercising faith in the Word, and thank God for this indescribable gift of godly fear. It is the power by which they persevere.

43. Bunyan, *The Holy War*, 283; see *Works*, 3:351.

44. Bunyan, *The Holy War*, 343; see *Works*, 3:371. The original reads, "'Twas I," instead of, "It was I."

Summary and Conclusion

John Bunyan delighted to fear the Lord. He said, "Thus you see what a weighty and great grace this grace of the holy fear of God is."[1] Bunyan feared God because He is God—the infinitely glorious Lord, beyond our comprehension. The only proper response to such a Being is awe and adoration. God is so inherently fearsome that one of His names is "the Fear of Isaac" (Gen. 31:42, 53). Sinful human beings can approach His holy majesty by faith in Jesus Christ alone, for Christ is the righteousness of sinners (see 2 Cor. 5:21). However, even when God comes to sinners in grace, His presence inspires awe (see Gen. 28:16–17). This is because God gives people a sense of His unspeakable majesty (see Rev. 15:4) and their horrible corruption (see Isa. 6:5).

The Lord is so beautiful and glorious that to see Him with an open heart is to love and fear Him. Even God's mercy—or, we should say, *especially* God's mercy—moves God's people to fear Him (see Hos. 3:5). It is wicked foolishness to worship God without a fearful

1. John Bunyan, *A Treatise of the Fear of God* (London: N. Ponder, 1679), 107; see *Works*, 1:462.

sense of His majesty; true worship is offered with both fear and joy (see Pss. 2:11; 5:7). Yet, by faith in the blood of Christ, it is not a fear of being condemned but a glad reverence (see Heb. 10:19–22).[2]

There are some kinds of fear toward God that do not please Him (see Ex. 20:20). The fallen human race, devoid of the Holy Spirit, still has a conscience that makes people aware of God and His judgments (see Rom. 2:14–15). This can produce fear of God that is ungodly fear, such as fear mixed with resentment, hiding from God, hypocrisy, seeking justification by works, or man-made forms of religion. There is another kind of fear of God that Bunyan said is godly for a time. In it, the Holy Spirit supernaturally applies God's Word to the conscience in order to awaken a fear of damnation (see John 16:8–9). It moves people to cry out, "What must I do to be saved?" (Acts 16:30), but in itself this fear saves no one. Salvation is by faith in Christ alone.

After a person trusts in Christ, the Holy Spirit no longer produces the fear of personal damnation, for the believer is now a child of God (see Rom. 8:15). When a sinner is saved, God's covenant guarantees that there is no condemnation for him ever again (see Rom. 8:1; Heb. 8:10–12). For a child of God to live under a sense of condemnation is for him to live in bondage to Satan's lies. True Christians who live in slavish fear of damnation will make it to heaven, but their road there will be much harder for themselves and for those around them.[3]

In contrast to ungodly fear and the fear of damnation, Bunyan said that there is a third kind of fear that is godly, even essential for salvation. It is a treasure given by God to His children, a fountain of life and wisdom (see Job 28:28; Prov. 14:27; Isa. 33:6). Fallen mankind does not have a spark of this godly fear (see Rom. 3:18), but God gives it to His chosen ones as a fruit of His covenant of grace

2. On the preceding two paragraphs, see chapter 3.
3. See chapter 4.

in Jesus Christ (see Jer. 32:40). This covenant is God's eternal will, in which He set the price of salvation as Christ's blood (see 1 Peter 1:19–20), the promise of salvation as the gift of eternal life (see Titus 1:2), and the people of salvation as those chosen by God (see Eph. 1:4).

The Holy Spirit applies Christ's saving work by giving a sinner a new heart with a childlike fear of God (see Isa. 11:2; Jer. 32:39). Far from a fear of punishment that mistrusts God's love (see 1 John 4:18), godly fear arises from a trust in God's mercy to sinners (see Ps. 130:3–4) and is mingled with love for God. Christians should not resist this fear but should cherish it and seek to excel in it (see Ps. 34:9). Growing in the fear of the Lord will keep them from much error and heartache (see Prov. 14:27; Eccl. 7:15–18). It makes a Christian honored, noble, strong, and above the control of the fear of mere men (see Prov. 31:30; Isa. 8:12–13; Luke 12:4–5).[4]

The fear of the Lord produces holy fruit. Bunyan taught that sinners are justified by faith in Christ alone and not by their works. However, justifying faith shows itself in the good works that it motivates and produces (see Titus 3:7–8). At the heart of becoming more holy is the fear of God (see 2 Cor. 7:1). It gives the believer the sense that he lives in God's presence and the submissiveness of heart to honor Him. The fear of God makes believers tender and zealous for God's glory (see 1 Sam. 17:26, 45). It moves them to hate sin (see Prov. 8:13) and to love obedience to God's law (see Ps. 112:1). Godly fear makes them watchful, prayerful, and worshipful. Those who fear the Lord deny themselves and serve others, even at their own expense or at risk of their lives (see 1 Kings 18:3–4; Neh. 5:15). Fear kills pride and nurtures hope in God's grace (see Ps. 147:11; Rom. 11:20).[5]

The great means by which God inculcates the fear of the Lord is the Holy Scriptures. God-fearing religion is biblical religion. The

4. See chapter 5.
5. See chapter 6.

Bible is not just a book about God; it is God's own voice in the world, and the voice of the Lord is full of majesty (see Ps. 29:4; 2 Tim. 3:16). It is the Scripture of truth, infallible and without error, and it cannot be broken (see Dan. 10:21; John 10:35). It has inherent authority to convince the mind, and it is the only foundation and standard for our religious beliefs. It is the supernatural mirror in which we can see into our own hearts and can see the glories and acts of Jesus Christ. It is sufficient to convert sinners and guide the godly (see Luke 16:29; 2 Tim. 3:14–17). Bunyan urged people to read the Bible, believe it, and obey it.

The fearsome quality of the Bible both exalts and humbles the ministry of the Word. On the one hand, it is a high and heavenly calling to preach the Scriptures to men. On the other hand, pastors are servants of the church, called to preach not themselves but Jesus Christ. Bunyan understood that the most gifted preacher is just a fiddle that Christ plays to make music for His church. Shall the fiddle boast? Far from it, for God will judge men not for their ability to preach, but for their reverent fear and obedience to the Word.[6]

In the end, the Christian life is not a performance on an earthly stage but a long-distance race requiring perseverance. Bunyan suffered greatly for his faith, and he both modeled perseverance and wrote of it. To encourage the saints, he reminded them that God gave many promises to those who fear the Lord. He is their Savior and Teacher (see Pss. 25:12; 115:11). He will defend them from evil (see Ps. 33:18–19) and delight them with the satisfaction of all their desires (see Pss. 34:9–10; 37:4). Best of all, God will give Himself to those who fear Him and will lavish His infinite love upon them forever and ever (see Ps. 103:11, 17).

Not only is the fear of God the mark that God puts on those whom He delights to bless, but it is also the means by which He

6. See chapter 7.

brings them to eternal happiness. The saints must persevere in order to enter into eternal glory with Christ (see Matt. 24:13). The Christian life is a thousand-mile marathon that must be run to gain the prize (see 1 Cor. 9:24). Christ therefore gives them all necessary grace so that every true believer will persevere (see John 6:37–39; Heb. 7:25). A key component of persevering grace is godly fear. God promised, "And I will make an everlasting covenant with them, that I will not turn away from them, to do them good; but I will put my fear in their hearts, that they shall not depart from me" (Jer. 32:40). Even when believers are lulled to sleep by spiritual laziness or besieged by temptations to sin, godly fear will wake them up and guard their hearts so that they will neither totally nor finally fall away.[7]

Bunyan's emphasis on the fear of the Lord instructs modern Christians as to their priorities. It is easy for a Christian to focus his attention on gifts, abilities, and skills by which to develop his personal kingdom, whether it is a household, a career, a business, or a church. As a result, those with great gifts or success can grow proud, and those with lesser ability or prosperity can get depressed. While gifts are desirable, and skill in our work is important, Bunyan reminds us that what really matters to God is that we fear Him. This will not lessen our zeal to serve Him but will purify our service of selfish and earthbound ends. It reminds us who is the King—whose kingdom and glory we must be seeking.

Christians may grow discouraged by their weaknesses and limitations, whether the lack of education, skill, ability, or opportunity, or the presence of disability, sickness, opposition, or religious persecution. Bunyan saw God's delight in holy fear to be a great encouragement to poor and suffering Christians. This grace does not require any status in the world or any great gifts and abilities. Those who are small in the eyes of men can excel in it. God will

7. See chapter 8.

bless those who fear Him, even the least and smallest of them (see Ps. 115:13), and He will reward the smallest of their acts of devotion to Him (see Matt. 10:42).[8] Bunyan wrote,

> This grace can make that man, that in many other things is not capable of serving of God, serve him better than those that have all, without it. Poor Christian man, you have scarce been able to do anything for God all your days, but only to fear the Lord. You are no preacher, and so cannot do him service that way. You are no rich man and so cannot do him service with outward substance. You are no wise man, and so cannot do anything that way. But here is your mercy, you fear God. Though you cannot preach, you can fear God. Though you have no bread to feed the belly nor fleece to cover the back of the poor, you can fear God.[9]

One imagines the tinker sitting in prison, unable to preach to his church, unable to care for his impoverished family, nevertheless thanking God for His inexpressible grace that has given him the fear of the Lord. He said, "Though this, to wit, that he fears the Lord, is all that he has in this world, he has the thing, the honor, the life, and glory that is lasting. His blessedness will abide when all men's but his is buried in the dust, in shame and contempt."[10]

These are sweet words of comfort for Christians who are bound and afflicted by circumstances beyond their control. Whether it is a child with few resources of his own, an old woman in a nursing home, the pastor of a struggling church, or a single parent overwhelmed by the demands of work and home, the Christian can fear the Lord. By a heart that fears the Lord, he can please God greatly. If you lead your family in the love and fear of the Lord, then you have given them something far more valuable than an abundance

8. Bunyan, *A Treatise of the Fear of God*, 152–55; see *Works*, 1:472.
9. Bunyan, *A Treatise of the Fear of God*, 229; see *Works*, 1:490.
10. Bunyan, *A Treatise of the Fear of God*, 231; see *Works*, 1:490.

of money and food (see Prov. 15:16–17). And who knows how God might take a seemingly insignificant but faithful Christian—one who truly fears the Lord—and use him to glorify God's holy name in the lives of others?

It is our hope that, after reading this book, you have seen the importance and tasted the goodness of the fear of the Lord. If you do not fear God as a believer in Christ and a child of the Father of glory, then you are in a terrifying predicament. You are lost, condemned, and enslaved in your sin. Even if you shrug off disturbing thoughts of God today, on the day of the Lord you will face the Holy Majesty, be judged for your sins, and be cast into hell. Why will you perish forever? Repent of your sins, trust in Jesus Christ, and learn from Him the fear of the Lord.

If you do fear God by faith in Christ, then nurture the fear of the Lord in your heart. Remember Bunyan's sound advice on how to grow in the fear of God. Keep watch over your heart and put sin to death at its first motions, lest it harden your heart. Beware too of slavish fear, the fear of rejection by God, for it is inappropriate and unhelpful for the justified child of God. Study the promises of God's covenant in Christ; they will teach you how to live as a reverent son or daughter of the living God. Grow in your assurance of salvation by exercising faith in Christ every day and walking in a good conscience before God and men. Meditate often on God's mercy and majesty, and on your own sin, so that your heart will be tender and humble. Immerse yourself in the Bible, and pray daily for your spiritual growth, that God would unite your heart to fear His name. If you are the head of a household, lead your family in family devotions. In all things, dedicate your life to fearing God with holy delight.[11]

"Blessed is every one that feareth the Lord!" (Ps. 128:1)

11. See the second part of chapter 6.

Bibliography

Ahenakaa, Anjov. "Justification and the Christian Life in John Bunyan: A Vindication of Bunyan from the Charge of Antinomianism." PhD Dissertation, Westminster Theological Seminary, Glenside, PA, 1997.

Alblas, Jacques B. H. "The Reception of *The Pilgrim's Progress* in Holland During the Eighteenth and Nineteenth Centuries." In *Bunyan in England and Abroad*, 121–30. Edited by M. Van Os and G. J. Schutte. Amsterdam: VU University Press, 1990.

Ambrose, Isaac. *Looking unto Jesus*. Pittsburgh: Luke Loomis, 1823.

Ames, William. *Conscience with the Power and Cases Thereof.* In *The Workes of the Reverend and Faithfull Minister of Christ William Ames*. London: John Rothwell, 1643.

———. *The Marrow of Sacred Divinity*. In *The Workes of the Reverend and Faithfull Minister of Christ William Ames*. London: John Rothwell, 1643.

Batson, E. Beatrice. "The Artistry of John Bunyan's Sermons." *Westminster Theological Journal* 38, no. 2 (Winter 1976): 166–81.

Bavinck, Herman. *Reformed Dogmatics*. Edited by John Bolt. Translated by John Vriend. 4 vols. Grand Rapids: Baker Academic, 2006.

Baxter, Richard. *A Christian Directory*. 1864. Reprint, Morgan, PA: Soli Deo Gloria, 1996.

Bayly, Lewis. *The Practice of Pietie*. London: Robert Allot, 1633.

———. *The Practice of Piety*. 1842. Reprint, Morgan, PA: Soli Deo Gloria, 1994.

Beeke, Joel R. "Bunyan's Perseverance." In *The Pure Flame of Devotion: The History of Christian Spirituality*. Edited by G. Stephen Weaver Jr. and Ian Hugh Clary. Kitchener, Ontario: Joshua Press, 2013.

———. "John Bunyan on Justification." *Midwestern Journal of Theology* 10, no. 1 (2011): 166–89.

———. *The Quest for Full Assurance: The Legacy of Calvin and His Successors*. Edinburgh, UK: Banner of Truth, 1999.

Beeke, Joel R., and Mark Jones. *A Puritan Theology: Doctrine for Life*. Grand Rapids: Reformation Heritage Books, 2012.

Beeke, Joel R., and Paul M. Smalley. *Prepared by Grace, for Grace: The Puritans on God's Ordinary Way of Leading Sinners to Christ*. Grand Rapids: Reformation Heritage Books, 2013.

Beeke, Joel R., and Randall J. Pederson. *Meet the Puritans*. Grand Rapids: Reformation Heritage Books, 2006.

Brown, John. *John Bunyan: His Life, Times, and Work*. London: Hulbert Publishing Co., 1928.

Bunyan, John. *The Acceptable Sacrifice: Or the Excellency of a Broken Heart*. London: George Larkin, 1689.

———. *The Barren Fig-Tree, Or, The Doom and Downfal of the Fruitless Professor*. London: Jonathan Robinson, 1673.

———. *Christian Behaviour; Being the Fruits of True Christianity*. 3rd ed. London: F. Smith, [1690].

———. *Come, and Welcome, to Jesus Christ*. 4th ed. London: by J. A. for John Harris, 1688.

———. *A Confession of My Faith, and A Reason of My Practice*. London: Francis Smith, 1672.

———. *A Defence of the Doctrine of Justification, By Faith in Jesus Christ Shewing, True Gospel-Holiness Flows from Thence*. London: Francis Smith, 1673.

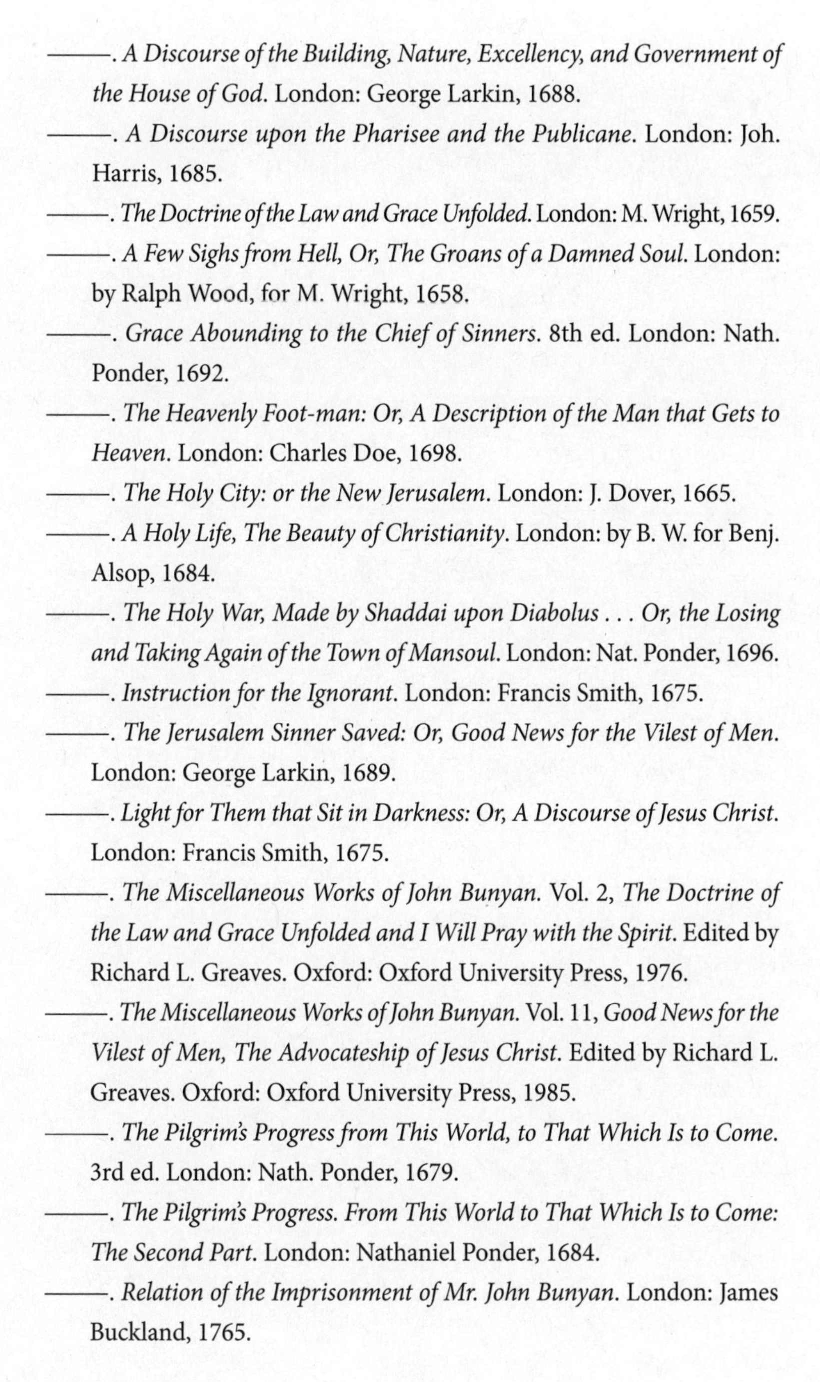

———. *A Discourse of the Building, Nature, Excellency, and Government of the House of God*. London: George Larkin, 1688.

———. *A Discourse upon the Pharisee and the Publicane*. London: Joh. Harris, 1685.

———. *The Doctrine of the Law and Grace Unfolded*. London: M. Wright, 1659.

———. *A Few Sighs from Hell, Or, The Groans of a Damned Soul*. London: by Ralph Wood, for M. Wright, 1658.

———. *Grace Abounding to the Chief of Sinners*. 8th ed. London: Nath. Ponder, 1692.

———. *The Heavenly Foot-man: Or, A Description of the Man that Gets to Heaven*. London: Charles Doe, 1698.

———. *The Holy City: or the New Jerusalem*. London: J. Dover, 1665.

———. *A Holy Life, The Beauty of Christianity*. London: by B. W. for Benj. Alsop, 1684.

———. *The Holy War, Made by Shaddai upon Diabolus . . . Or, the Losing and Taking Again of the Town of Mansoul*. London: Nat. Ponder, 1696.

———. *Instruction for the Ignorant*. London: Francis Smith, 1675.

———. *The Jerusalem Sinner Saved: Or, Good News for the Vilest of Men*. London: George Larkin, 1689.

———. *Light for Them that Sit in Darkness: Or, A Discourse of Jesus Christ*. London: Francis Smith, 1675.

———. *The Miscellaneous Works of John Bunyan*. Vol. 2, *The Doctrine of the Law and Grace Unfolded and I Will Pray with the Spirit*. Edited by Richard L. Greaves. Oxford: Oxford University Press, 1976.

———. *The Miscellaneous Works of John Bunyan*. Vol. 11, *Good News for the Vilest of Men, The Advocateship of Jesus Christ*. Edited by Richard L. Greaves. Oxford: Oxford University Press, 1985.

———. *The Pilgrim's Progress from This World, to That Which Is to Come*. 3rd ed. London: Nath. Ponder, 1679.

———. *The Pilgrim's Progress. From This World to That Which Is to Come: The Second Part*. London: Nathaniel Ponder, 1684.

———. *Relation of the Imprisonment of Mr. John Bunyan*. London: James Buckland, 1765.

———. *The Resurrection of the Dead and Eternal Judgment*. London: Francis Smith, ca. 1665.

———. *Some Gospel-Truths Opened*. London: J. Wright, 1656.

———. *A Treatise of the Fear of God*. London: N. Ponder, 1679.

———. *A Vindication of the Book Called, Some Gospel-Truths Opened*. London: Matthias Cowley, 1657.

———. *The Water of Life*. London: Nathanael Ponder, 1688.

———. *The Work of Jesus Christ as an Advocate*. London: Dorman Newman, 1688.

———. *The Works of John Bunyan*. Edited by George Offor. 3 vols. 1854. Reprint, Edinburgh, UK: Banner of Truth, 1991.

———. *The Works of that Eminent Servant of Christ Mr. John Bunyan*. 2 vols. 3rd ed. London: W. Johnston, 1767.

———. *The Works of that Eminent Servant of Christ Mr. John Bunyan, the First Volume*. London: William Marshall, 1692. Bunyan's writings cited from this volume include:

Christ a Compleat Saviour: Or the Intercession of Christ, and Who Are Privileged in It.

The Desire of the Righteous Granted.

Exposition on the Ten First Chapters of Genesis, and Part of the Eleventh.

Justification by an Imputed Righteousness. Or, No Way to Heaven but by Jesus Christ.

Of the Law and a Christian.

A Mapp Shewing the Order and Causes of Salvation and Damnation.

Paul's Departure and Crown.

The Saints Knowledge of Christ's Love, Or, The Unsearchable Riches of Christ.

The Saints' Privilege and Profit.

Saved by Grace: Or, A Discourse of the Grace of God.

Calhoun, David B. *Grace Abounding: The Life, Books, and Influence of John Bunyan*. Ross-shire, UK: Christian Focus Publications, 2005.

Calvin, John. *Institutes of the Christian Religion*. Edited by John T. McNeill. Translated by Ford Lewis Battles. The Library of Christian Classics 20, 21. Philadelphia: Westminster Press, 1960.

Campbell, Gordon. "The Source of Bunyan's *Mapp of Salvation*." *Journal of the Warburg and Courtauld Institutes* 44 (1981): 240–41.

Cook, Faith. *Fearless Pilgrim: The Life and Times of John Bunyan*. Darlington, UK: Evangelical Press, 2008.

Denne, Henry. *The Quaker no Papist, in Answer to The Quaker Disarmed*. London: Francis Smith, 1659.

Dennison, James T., Jr., ed. *Reformed Confessions of the Sixteenth and Seventeenth Centuries in English Translation*. Vol. 2, *1552–1566*. Grand Rapids: Reformation Heritage Books, 2010.

———. *Reformed Confessions of the Sixteenth and Seventeenth Centuries in English Translation*. Vol. 4, *1600–1693*. Grand Rapids: Reformation Heritage Books, 2014.

De Vries, Pieter. *John Bunyan on the Order of Salvation*. Translated by C. van Haaften. New York: Peter Lang, 1994.

Dod, John and Robert Cleaver. *A Plaine and Familiar Exposition of the Ten Commaundements*. London: by Humfrey Lownes for Thomas Man, 1606.

Doe, Charles. "The Struggler." In *The Works of that Eminent Servant of Christ Mr. John Bunyan, the First Volume*. London: William Marshall, 1692.

Duckett, George, ed. *Penal Laws and Test Act: Questions Touching Their Repeal Propounded in 1687–8 by James II*. London, 1883.

Edwards, Jonathan. "'Catalogue' of Reading." In *The Works of Jonathan Edwards*. Vol. 26, *Catalogues of Books*. Edited by Peter J. Thuesen. New Haven, CT: Yale University Press, 2008.

———. *Religious Affections*. In *The Works of Jonathan Edwards*. Vol. 2, *Religious Affections*. Edited by John E. Smith. New Haven, CT: Yale University Press, 1959.

Fisher, Edward. *The Marrow of Modern Divinity*. London: by R. W. for G. Calvert, 1645.

———. *The Marrow of Modern Divinity*. Edited by Thomas Boston. Ross-shire, UK: Christian Focus Publications, 2009.

Frank, Arnold. *The Fear of God, A Forgotten Doctrine: Learning from Puritan Preaching*. Ventura, CA: Nordskog, 2007.

Greaves, Richard L. "Bunyan, John." In *Oxford Dictionary of National Biography*, 8:702–11. Oxford: Oxford University Press, 2004.

———. *Glimpses of Glory: John Bunyan and English Dissent*. Stanford, CA: Stanford University Press, 2002.

———. *John Bunyan*. Courtenay Studies in Reformation Theology 2. Grand Rapids: Eerdmans, 1969.

———. "John Bunyan and Covenant Thought in the Seventeenth Century." *Church History* 36, no. 2 (June 1967): 151–69.

Green, Jay. "Bunyan, John." In *The Encyclopedia of Christianity*, 2:220–28. Edited by Gary G. Cohen. Marshalltown, DE: The National Foundation for Christian Education, 1968.

Haykin, Michael A. G. *Kiffin, Knollys, and Keach: Rediscovering Our English Baptist Heritage*. Leeds, UK: Reformation Trust Today, 1996.

Hill, Christopher. *A Tinker and a Poor Man: John Bunyan and His Church, 1628–1688*. New York: Alfred A. Knopf, 1989.

Hodge, Charles. *Systematic Theology*. 3 vols. Reprint, Peabody, MA: Hendrickson, 1999.

Hooker, Thomas. *The Soules Preparation for Christ*. The Netherlands: n.p., 1638.

Ivimey, Joseph. *A History of the English Baptists*. Vol. 2. London: for the author, 1814.

Keeble, N. H. *The Literary Culture of Nonconformity in Later Seventeenth-Century England*. Leicester, UK: Leicester University Press, 1987.

Knott, John R., Jr. "'Thou must live upon my Word': Bunyan and the Bible." In *John Bunyan: Conventicle and Parnassus; Tercentenary Essays*. Edited by N. H. Keeble. Oxford, UK: Clarendon Press, 1988.

Luther, Martin. *A Commentarie of Master Doctor Martin Luther upon the Epistle of S. Paul to the Galathians*. London: George Miller, 1644.

Macauley, J. S. "Gifford, John." In *Biographical Dictionary of British Radicals in the Seventeenth Century*, 2:9. Edited by Richard L. Greaves and Robert Zaller. Brighton, UK: Harvester, 1983.

Muller, Richard A. *Dictionary of Latin and Greek Theological Terms: Drawn Principally from Protestant Scholastic Theology*. Grand Rapids: Baker, 1985.

Nuttall, Geoffrey F. "Review of *The Miscellaneous Works of John Bunyan, Volume IX, A Treatise of the Fear of God; The Greatness of the Soul; A Holy Life*. Edited by Richard L. Greaves." *Religious Studies* 18, no. 4 (December 1982): 549–51.

Owen, John. *The Doctrine of Justification by Faith*. In *The Works of John Owen*. Vol. 5. Edited by William H. Goold. 1850–1853. Reprint, Edinburgh, UK: Banner of Truth, 1965.

———. *The Doctrine of the Saints' Perseverance Explained and Confirmed*. In *The Works of John Owen*. Vol. 11. Edited by William H. Goold. 1850–1853. Reprint, Edinburgh, UK: Banner of Truth, 1965.

Owens, W. R. "John Bunyan and the Bible." In *The Cambridge Companion to Bunyan*. Edited by Anne Dunan-Page. Cambridge, UK: Cambridge University Press, 2010.

———. "The Reception of *The Pilgrim's Progress* in England." In *Bunyan in England and Abroad*, 91–104. Edited by M. Van Os and G. J. Schutte. Amsterdam: VU University Press, 1990.

Owst, Gerald R. *Literature and Pulpit in Medieval England*. Cambridge: Cambridge University Press, 1933.

Perkins, William. *An Exposition of the Symbole or Creed of the Apostles*. London: John Legat, 1595.

———. *A Golden Chaine, Or The Description of Theologie, Containing the Order of the Causes of Salvation and Damnation, According to God's Word*. London: John Legate, 1597.

———. *The Whole Treatise of the Cases of Conscience*. London: John Legat, 1606.

Richey, Robert A. "The Puritan Doctrine of Sanctification: Constructions of the Saints' Final Perseverance and Complete Perseverance as Mirrored in Bunyan's 'The Pilgrim's Progress.'" ThD Dissertation. Mid-America Baptist Theological Seminary, Schenectady, NY, 1990.

Rivers, Isabel. "Grace, Holiness, and the Pursuit of Happiness: Bunyan and Restoration Latitudinarianism." In *John Bunyan: Conventicle and Parnassus; Tercentenary Essays*. Edited by N. H. Keeble. Oxford: Clarendon Press, 1988.

Smith, Thomas. *A Gagg for the Quakers, with an Answer to Mr. Denn's Quaker No Papist*. London: J. C., 1659.

———. *The Quaker Disarm'd, or A True Relation of a Late Public Dispute Held at Cambridge . . . With A Letter in Defence of the Ministry, and against Lay-Preachers*. London: J. C., 1659.

Spurgeon, C. H. *The Metropolitan Tabernacle Pulpit*. Vol. 45. 1899. Reprint, Pasadena, TX: Pilgrim Publications, 1977.

Sternhold, Thomas, John Hopkins, et al. *The Whole Booke of Psalmes: Collected into English Meeter*. London: by G. M. for the Company of Stationers, 1644.

Thomas Aquinas. *Summa Theologica, Part 2 (First Part)*. Translated by the Fathers of the English Dominican Province. London: R. & T. Washbourne, 1915.

Wakefield, Gordon S. "Bunyan and the Christian Life." In *John Bunyan: Conventicle and Parnassus; Tercentenary Essays*. Edited by N. H. Keeble. Oxford: Clarendon Press, 1988.

Walton, Brad. *Jonathan Edwards,* Religious Affections *and the Puritan Analysis of True Piety, Spiritual Sensation and Heart Religion*. Studies in American Religion 74. Lewiston, NY: Edwin Mellen Press, 2002.

White, B. R. "Denne, Henry." In *Biographical Dictionary of British Radicals in the Seventeenth Century*, 1:223. Edited by Richard L. Greaves and Robert Zaller. Brighton, UK: Harvester, 1982.

Whitefield, George. Preface to *The Works of that Eminent Servant of Christ Mr. John Bunyan*, 1:iii–iv. 2 vols. 3rd ed. London: W. Johnston, 1767.